Sayings and Doings of Pai-chang

Ch'an Master of Great Wisdom

This book was donated by

Robert L. Nugent, Ph.D.

Professor Emeritus
of Modern Languages
and former Director
of the James F. Lincoln Library

ZEN WRITINGS SERIES
Center Publications Los Angeles, California

SAYINGS AND DOINGS OF PAI-CHANG

Ch'an Master of Great Wisdom

Translated from the Chinese by Thomas Cleary

This three-circle logo is the trademark of Center Publications, publishers of fine books on Zen, Buddhism, the arts, comparative religion and related fields. Director: John Daido Loori. Editor/assistant director: Stephan Ikko Bodian. Production manager/designer: Larry Watson. Title page calligraphy: Gerow Reece.

Related titles available from
Center Publications, 905 S. Normandie Ave., Los Angeles, CA 90006

THE WAY OF EVERYDAY LIFE
by Hakuyu Taizan Maezumi
Photography by John Daido Loori, paper $9.95, cloth $17.50
A unique collaboration of words and images expresses the poetic vision of the enlightened life.

HOW TO RAISE AN OX
by Francis Dojun Cook, $5.95
Translations and interpretations of ten practice-oriented chapters of Zen Master Dogen's masterwork, *Shobogenzo*.

GATELESS GATE
by Kohun Yamada, paper $6.95, cloth $13.50
A new translation of the classic koan collection, *Mumonkan*. Kohun Yamada Roshi's concise commentaries—originally delivered in English to his western students—point straight to the heart of each koan, leaving no room for vague abstraction.

TO FORGET THE SELF: An Illustrated Guide to Zen Meditation
by John Daishin Buksbazen, $7.95
An artistic, conversational and authoritative guide to Zen meditation, with the most detailed instructions available.

THE HAZY MOON OF ENLIGHTENMENT: On Zen Practice III
by Hakuyu Taizan Maezumi and Bernard Tetsugen Glassman, $4.95
Two contemporary Zen teachers take a penetrating look at the teaching of enlightenment, the path leading to it, and the delusions which obscure it.

ON ZEN PRACTICE: Foundations of Practice
ON ZEN PRACTICE II: Body, Breath and Mind
Edited by Hakuyu Taizan Maezumi and Bernard Tetsugen Glassman, $4.00 each
Collected essays, teaching stories, discourses, and illustrations bring the fundamentals of Zen practice alive in the context of contemporary American life.

SAYINGS AND DOINGS OF PAI-CHANG, PUBLISHED UNDER THE JOINT AUSPICES OF THE ZEN CENTER OF LOS ANGELES AND THE INSTITUTE FOR TRANSCULTURAL STUDIES, IS ONE VOLUME IN THE ZEN WRITINGS SERIES, A MONOGRAPHIC SUBSCRIPTION SERIES COMPRISING TWO NEW TITLES EACH YEAR. SUBSCRIPTION RATE FOR ONE YEAR: $10.00 IN THE U.S. AND CANADA, $15.00 FOREIGN. FOR TWO YEARS: $20.00 IN THE U.S. AND CANADA, $30.00 FOREIGN.

FOR FURTHER INFORMATION, CONTACT: CENTER PUBLICATIONS, 905 S. NORMANDIE AVENUE, LOS ANGELES, CA 90006. © 1978 BY ZEN CENTER OF LOS ANGELES, INC. PRINTED IN THE UNITED STATES OF AMERICA.

LIBRARY OF CONGRESS CATALOGUING IN PUBLICATION DATA:

HUAI-HAI, SHIH, 720–814.
   SAYINGS AND DOINGS OF PAI-CHANG.

   (ZEN WRITINGS SERIES; 6)
   BIBLIOGRAPHY: P.
   CONTENTS: INTRODUCTION.—RECORD OF SAYINGS OF THE MEDITATION MASTER OF GREAT WISDOM WHO LIVED ON PAI-CHANG MOUNTAIN IN HUNG-CHOU.—EXTENSIVE RECORD OF PAI-CHANG.
   1. ZEN BUDDHISM—EARLY WORKS TO 1800. I. CLEARY, THOMAS F., 1949– II. HUAI-HAI, SHIH, 720–814. HUNG-CHOU PAI-CHANG SHAN TA-CHIH CH'AN SHIH YU LU. ENGLISH. 1979. III. HUAI-HAI, SHIH, 720–814. PAI-CHANG KUANG LU. ENGLISH. 1979. IV. TITLE. V. SERIES: THE ZEN WRITINGS SERIES; 6.
BQ9299.H833E5 1978   294.3'927   78-21228
ISBN 0-916820-10-6

ACKNOWLEDGEMENTS

This translation of the teachings of Pai-chang Huai-hai was originally presented as part of a PhD. thesis at Harvard University; thanks are due to Professor Masatoshi Nagatomi and to Professor Lien-sheng Yang, and to the staff of the Harvard Yenching library.

CONTENTS

INTRODUCTION
1

RECORD OF SAYINGS OF THE MEDITATION MASTER OF GREAT WISDOM (WHO LIVED ON) PAI-CHANG MOUNTAIN IN HUNG-CHOU
17

EXTENSIVE RECORD OF PAI-CHANG
29

BIBLIOGRAPHY
85

FOOTNOTES
89

INTRODUCTION

Pai-chang Huai-hai (720–814) is one of the most celebrated of the ancient teachers of Ch'an (Zen) Buddhism, especially honored as the founder of the Ch'an meditation commune in T'ang dynasty China. Pai-chang also transmitted the inner message of Ch'an through numerous successors, and his sayings and doings have subsequently been scattered throughout the teaching lore of Ch'an and its offspring schools throughout East Asia.

According to the Sung dynasty *Biographies of Eminent Monks*, Pai-chang Huai-hai was a man from Min, that is Fu-chou or Fukien, and "when young he departed from the 'rotten house' and long sojourned in the sudden school;" that is he left his home and society and became a monk when he was still a youth, and studied Ch'an Buddhism for a long time; "his endowment was by nature, and did not come from being urged on." When the great master Ma-tsu, "Ancestor Ma," was beginning to teach in Nan-k'ang in Chiang-hsi, Huai-hai went there; according to the biography, "He went empty and returned fulfilled, and ultimately became a master of the school." The story of Pai-chang's awakening and some of his dialogues with Ma-tsu are told in the record of Pai-chang's sayings.

According to the *Annals of the Forest* by the distinguished Sung dynasty Ch'an master-literatus Chiao-fen, after the death of Ancestor Ma, Pai-chang ended his pilgrimage and came back to sit at the great teacher's tomb. There seekers of the Way eventually came to learn from Pai-chang. The *Biographies of Eminent Monks* continues, "Later generous believers invited him to live in the Hsin-wu region (of Chiang-hsi)—there was a mountain there, extremely steep, about ten thousand feet high, (named Ta-hsiung, but) called Pai-chang (as an epithet). Once Huai-hai was dwelling there, Ch'an students came without regard for distance; the halls and rooms were too small to hold them all."

Eventually Pai-chang Huai-hai established a new monastic code for the community, which subsequently became a guide for other Ch'an schools. According to *Biographies of Eminent Monks*,

> (Pai-chang) encompassed the great and lesser vehicles, synthesizing them to set up standards, striving to bring them back to good. Thus as an innovator, he did not follow the regulations of the Indian monastic code, but set up a special Ch'an abode.
>
> Since the transmission of the teaching beginning from Bodhidharma reached the sixth patriarch, those who attained the eye of the Way were called Great Elder, the same as how those in India who were exalted in the Way were called *Acharya*.

> However, they mostly dwelt in monasteries of the schools of precepts, their only distinction being that they dwelt in separate buildings. Pai-chang had them all enter a monks' hall, without regard to high or low.

Pai-chang organized a service elite instead of a cloistered and privileged elite, with the process of the teaching being carried out through the fabric of the community. The austere life of work and study among the "mountain monks" of the Ch'an schools was for centuries an underlying source of civilization and human culture in China, providing not only means of direct knowledge and inspiration, but also working models for the accomplishment of individual and common weal in a differentiated yet egalitarian society. The *Biographies of Eminent Monks* continues its description of the Ch'an monks' hall:

> In the hall were set up long continuous benches, and shelves for utensils. When lying down, they would always do so on their sides, pillowed on the edge of the bench; this is called "sleeping with a sword on." Only because their sitting meditation was long, they just lay down for a little while, that's all.
>
> They inquired in the mornings and assembled at night. They ate and drank in moderation, showing frugality; they practiced the rule of communal work, showing that high and low must equally exert their strength.

Ch'an teachings humanized Chinese Buddhism, emphasizing practical application beyond theory, without maintaining or emphasizing an idealized image of superhuman Buddhahood. This was reflected in humanitarian works of charity, education, and service in the world, as well as in the special function of awakening the basic inner illumination of the human mind that is the source knowledge of Ch'an. Even Pai-chang's very organization manifestly emphasized the necessity of suiting the teaching to current needs, and not allowing it to become dead words. The great elder of the community, the guide, "dwelt in a ten-foot square room, the same as Vimalakirti's single room," alluding to a famous Buddhist scripture in which an enlightened layman, Vimalakirti, demonstrates nonduality of delusion and enlightenment by being a Buddha "in the world yet not stained by the things of the world." Thus, "Pai-chang did not set up a Buddha shrine, only a teaching (Dharma) hall, to show that the teaching goes beyond words and images."

Thus Pai-chang's work was a major evolutionary step in the development of Ch'an activity in China, even as his teaching style is also known for marking the transition of the Ch'an teaching from principle to fact. The *Biographies of Eminent Monks* concludes,

> Various regulations of his were antithetical to the teachers of the (Indian) monastic codes; the Ch'an schools all over the land followed his example like grass bending in the wind. The independent practice of the Ch'an school began from Pai-chang Huai-hai.

Pai-chang was a successor in the ninth generation of a Buddhist teaching line that appeared in China around the turn of the sixth century A.D. with the Indian Buddhist yogi Bodhidharma, who is said to have been directed by the twenty-seventh Buddhist patriarch, Prajnatara, to go to China after teaching in India for fifty years.

When Bodhidharma came to China in the late fifth century, Buddhist studies were flourishing in China, but according to tradition the only scripture he used was the *Mahayanalanka-avatara* [The entry of the great vehicle into Srilanka (Ceylon)], a compendium of teachings of the Yogacara or yoga-practice school, which is also known as the "consciousness only" school, teaching that what we conceive of as reality is actually just mental construction projected on faculties, consciousness, and data of sense, which are only real relative to each other, and thus have no fixed nature of their own. Various yogic practices are used, therefore, to break down the illusion of the ultimate reality of any description and free the mind from attachment to habitual patterns of thought.

Bodhidharma is said to have spent some fifty years traveling and teaching in various parts of China, and various collections of sayings are attributed to him. The most widely accepted of these, that which is of earliest record, is the well-known outline of two kinds of entry into the Way, recorded in the T'ang dynasty *Biographies of Eminent Monks* as follows:

> There are many roads of entry into the Way, but they are essentially of only two kinds, called principle and action. Realizing the source by way of the teachings, one deeply believes that all living beings have the same unique real nature: but since it is veiled by outside elements, one brings about the abandonment of falsehood and return to reality, freezing and abiding in "wall-gazing," with no self or other, ordinary and holy being equal, the same; firmly abiding without moving, not following other persuasions, tacitly merging with the Way, silently not-doing, is called entry by principle.
>
> In the four practices of entry by action, myriad practices are likewise included.

The first is the practice of compensation for opposition: in cultivating the Way, when beset by suffering, one should think of times past when one abandoned the root and pursued the branches, giving rise to much love and hate; though now one may have committed no transgression, he has himself done so in the past, so he accepts it contentedly without any resentment or complaint at all. A scripture speaks of encountering suffering without anxiety; this is because of perfect knowledge. When this mind is produced, it has no discord with the Way, because by thoroughly comprehending opposition one advances on the path.

The second is the practice of according with conditions. Sentient beings have no self; pain and pleasure are according to conditions. Even if one obtains such things as prosperity and fame, they are what was made by past causes, and are only now realized—when the conditions are exhausted, they return to nothing. So what is there to rejoice about? Gain or loss are according to conditions; there is no increase or decrease in the mind. When adverse and favorable winds are still, one tacitly accords with truth.

The third is called the practice of having no object of seeking. Worldly people wander forever, attached by greed here and there; this is called "seeking." Heroes of the Way are aware that the true principle is contrary to the mundane; with their minds at ease, without striving, their forms go along with the turns of fate. The world is all suffering; who can find ease? A scripture says that to have any seeking is all suffering, and absence of seeking is bliss.

The fourth is called the practice of conforming with truth; this is the truth of the purity of nature.

Bodhidharma's teaching transcended the conventions of the day, and he was poisoned on several occasions by rival preachers; according to the *Biographies of Eminent Monks*,

Bodhidharma taught meditation wherever he stayed; at that time, the country was full of the lecturing profession, and when they heard his method of still meditation, many began to talk against him.

Bodhidharma had several adept pupils, among whom Hui-k'e (486–593) is known as the second patriarch of Ch'an, the foremost enlightened disciple of the patriarch Bodhidharma. Hui-k'e had studied Confucian, Taoist, and Buddhist classics, then became a monk and practiced meditation according to the Buddhist teachings for eight years before he finally met Bodhidharma at the Shao-lin monastery near Lo-yang in northwest China around 526 A.D.

It is well known that Hui-k'e had only one arm; the *Biographies of Eminent Monks* says that it was cut off by outlaws, but Ch'an tradition has it that he "presented his severed arm" to Bodhidharma, who said, "All the Buddhas, in the very beginning of their search for the Way, forget their bodies for the sake of the Truth." It is said that this gesture of renunciation by Hui-k'e made Bodhidharma realize that he was a true vessel of teaching, and prompted him to assist Hui-k'e in his search for enlightenment.

Subsequently Hui-k'e asked Bodhidharma to set his mind at peace for him. Bodhidharma said, "Bring me your mind and I will set it at peace." Hui-k'e said, "When I look for my mind, I can't grasp it." Bodhidharma said, "I have set your mind at peace." At these words Hui-k'e was awakened. This famous and oft-repeated story illustrates a critical point in meditation: according to a meditation system of T'ien-t'ai Buddhism, looking for the mind itself is the next step after the cessation of thought and the exercise of analytic insight; it is designed to conduct the mind from contemplative insight to spontaneous realization of the inherently pure nature of mind and things.

Hui-k'e stayed with Bodhidharma for six years, then, according to the *Biographies of Eminent Monks*, went into the ordinary world to test the power of his realization. In 534 he went into the metropolis of Yeh in Honan, in a northern Chinese state, where he taught for thirty years. In his latter years, after the persecution of Buddhism by Emperor Wu of the Northern Chou dynasty in 575, Hui-k'e gave up the outward form of a monk forever after having been defrocked, and mingled with the populace. Like Bodhidharma, Hui-k'e incurred the opposition of other Buddhist preachers, and was finally put to death, even though over a hundred years old, as the result of an intrigue. Hui-k'e is said to have produced as many as ten enlightened disciples, including several laymen, among whom was the mysterious Seng-ts'an.

There is hardly any record of the third patriarch of Ch'an, Seng-ts'an (d.606). A man of unknown origins and said to be a leper, he was a middle-aged layman when he met Hui-k'e. After the persecution of Buddhism in northern China, Seng-ts'an hid in the mountains of central China, living in no fixed place. According to an early Ch'an history known as the *Record of Teachers and Students of the Lanka-avatara*, Seng-ts'an kept his realization secret and transmitted Ch'an only to one man. Tradition also ascribes a long poem to Seng-ts'an, the first work of Ch'an literature; it is quoted several times by Pai-chang, and has been a favorite Ch'an text as far back as its history is known.

According to the record of the fourth patriarch Tao-hsin (580–651) in the *Biographies of Eminent Monks*, "There were two monks—no one knew where they had come from—who went into Yuan-kung mountain in Anhwei province and quietly practiced meditation. Tao-hsin heard of them and went there and received instruction; he studied there for ten years." This meeting took place when Tao-hsin was in his youth; the two monks were Hui-k'e and Seng-ts'an.

The teaching career of the fourth patriarch was a landmark in Ch'an history, as he opened an independent teaching center on a mountain and settled there for thirty years to teach, the community of students eventually swelling to over five hundred people. The *Teachers and Students of the Lanka-avatara* says, "He reopened the gate of Ch'an, and it circulated throughout the land." The independence of Tao-hsin's community was cemented by his refusal to go to the capital as a national teacher when summoned by the imperial throne. Tao-hsin also formulated precepts for the community, in this respect also being the forerunner of Pai-chang, who was once again to give the Ch'an monastery independent life some two hundred and fifty years later.

Tao-hsin also compiled a volume of instructions for meditation, in which, according to the *Record of Teachers and Students of the Lanka-avatara*, the methods he employed were generally of five major types:

1) "Knowing the essence of the mind; its intrinsic essence is pure clarity, it is essentially the same as a Buddha."
2) "Knowing the function of the mind; its function produces the treasure of

Dharma; its activity always silent, myriad delusions are all thus."

3) "Always be aware, without stopping; the aware mind being present, it senses the formlessness of things."
4) "Always seeing the body as empty and quiet, inside and outside communing in sameness; plunging the body into the realm of reality, there has never been any hindrance."
5) "Keeping to one without shifting; in motion and stillness always there, enabling the student to clearly see the enlightened nature."

Several examples are also given in the text of the *Record of Teachers and Students of the Lanka-avatara:*

> Constantly be mindful of the six senses empty and still, always like the middle of the night. That which is seen and heard during the day are all things outside the body; inside the body is always empty and pure. To maintain oneness without wavering, with this pure eye, concentrate the eyes on one thing; without question of the time of day or night, concentrate your mind constantly, without moving: when your mind wants to run off in confusion, quickly grab it and bring it back under control.
>
> It is like tying a bird's legs; when it wants to fly, you tether and restrain it. Spending days gazing without ceasing, the mind, subdued, will become settled of itself.

Tao-hsin also recommended repetition of the name of a Buddha as a technique to develop mental focus, then finally identified "remembrance of Buddha" (*nien-fo*, a name for the practice of invocation of a Buddha name) with "remembrance of mind" (*nien-hsin*), and "remembrance of mind" with "nothing on the mind" (*wu-so-nien*). He concludes, "If you realize that the mind is fundamentally unborn and does not perish and is ultimately pure and clear, this itself is the pure Buddha land."

Tao-hsin emphasized the proper balance of practices which halt conception and practices involving contemplation, analysis, and observation; he said, "If you always remain in the stopped mind, you'll sink into oblivion; if you stay too long in the observing mind, you'll become scattered." He states that a Ch'an adept is not affected by either stillness or disturbance; regarding the process, he says,

> An enlightened being in the beginning stage first realizes that all is empty; later he realizes that all is not empty: this is nondiscriminating wisdom. It is also (what is meant by) "form itself is empty." It is not emptiness (as a result of) the annihilation of form; the very nature of form is empty. The practice of enlightening beings has emptiness as its realization: when beginning students see emptiness, this is seeing emptiness, it is not real emptiness. Those who cultivate the Way and attain real emptiness do not see emptiness or nonemptiness; they have no views.

Tao-hsin himself is said to have sat in meditation for sixty years without ever lying down. He insisted that the course of mind must be clear and discernment complete before ever presuming to teach others, that knowledge of individual students' states and potentials is essential to teacherhood. This characteristic Buddhist teaching was put into effect by the Ch'an folk in China, this being the reason for the great number and variety of Ch'an texts, and the fluidity for which it has been called adogmatic or iconoclastic, the teaching beyond doctrine.

Tao-hsin named only one successor, Hung-jen (602–675), who thus became known as the fifth patriarch of Ch'an. Hung-jen was a native of the Huang-mei district of Hupei, where the fourth patriarch was teaching; he began to attend Tao-hsin at the age of seven, and stayed with him for thirty years. According to the *Record of the Treasure of the Teaching in Successive Generations,* Hung-jen always worked diligently at chores, and at night would sit in meditation until dawn. When he became a teacher and inherited the robe and bowl of Bodhidharma, he moved to the other of the twin peaks of the mountain where Tao-hsin taught. Hung-jen eventually led a community of seven hundred people, and had eleven enlightened disciples.

Hui-neng (638–713), the sixth and perhaps most famous patriarch of Ch'an, was an illiterate orphan who was suddenly awakened in his mid-twenties when he happened to hear a certain line of well-known scripture as he sold firewood in a market of Canton. While the fifth patriarch had also been an illiterate orphan, from the age of seven he was raised by the most learned and cultivated people in China; Hui-neng, on the other hand, was what cultured society (even monastic society) considered a rude barbarian, "unable even to pronounce words correctly." The transmission of the mind seal to Hui-neng was shocking to the community at first, but later was widely appreciated as emblematic of the universality of the reality behind Ch'an. When two of Hung-jen's enlightened heirs, Shen-hsiu (602–706) and Hui-an (580–707) came to teach in the capital of China at the request of the sovereign Empress

Wu, both openly acknowledged Hui-neng as the greatest Ch'an master of the age, endowed with the "wisdom that has no teacher."

Already recognized as an enlightened being after his first awakening in the market place, Hui-neng was given a temple to live and preach in, but before long he left that situation to go meet the fifth patriarch. After eight months as a workman in Hung-jen's community, Hui-neng was given the robe and bowl of Bodhidharma and sent away in the middle of night. For fifteen years he wandered anonymously through mountains and forests in the company of hunters, eventually to re-emerge in south China, becoming the most familiar of the great Ch'an patriarchs.

Hui-neng is said to have taught thirty-three enlightened successors who appeared in the world, ten great hidden ones, and also innumerable people of all kinds who were awakened by his teaching. Many of the disciples were monks of high attainment in the doctrinal and Ch'an schools already, one was even a canonical master from India; the frequent records of sudden enlightenments which characterize the school of Hui-neng must be understood against a background of intense effort in application of the Buddhist teachings and an advanced level of mental cultivation. Hui-neng's teachings, such as they have come down to posterity, are known for their great simplicity, often spoken from the standpoint of effect:

> Good friends, wisdom observes and illumines inside and outside, clearly penetrating and perceiving your own fundamental mind: if you know the fundamental mind, that is original liberation; if you realize liberation, that is wisdom and concentration. This is just no thought. What is no thought? If you see all things without your mind being affected or attached, this

is no thought. When you use it, it extends everywhere, yet without being attached anywhere.

Just purify the basic mind, and let the six consciousnesses go out through the six (sense-) gates into the six (data-) fields, without any defilement or mix-up therein; coming and going freely, functioning everywhere without tarrying anywhere is wisdom and concentration. Freedom and liberation is called the practice of no thought. If you do not think of anything at all, and keep thought always cut off, this is the bondage of Dharma, and is called a biased view.

Good friends, if you would cultivate imperturbability, just whenever you see people, do not see their right or wrong, good or bad, faults or troubles; then your own nature is immovable. Good friends, even though the bodies of deluded people be immobile, yet when they open their mouths they speak of the right and wrong, strengths and weaknesses, good and bad of other people—they turn away from the path. If you cling to mind or cling to purity, this veils the path.

What is called sitting meditation? In this way there is no obstruction, no impediment. When outwardly, in the midst of all pleasant or unpleasant realms, thoughts do not arise in the mind, this is called "sitting." Inwardly to see that one's own nature does not move is called "meditation."

Introduction

Very few of Hui-neng's disciples had any successors of their own in turn, and little is known of any of them. From the perspective of subsequent Ch'an history, the two most important successors of the sixth patriarch were Ch'ing-yuan Hsing-ssu (d.740) and Nan-yueh Huai-jang (677–744). Little is known of these two men themselves, but their respective successors, Shih-t'ou Hsi-ch'ien (700–799) and Ma-tsu Tao-i (709–788) became the foremost Ch'an teachers of the age, known as the two "gates of elixir." According to the standard Ch'an history *Transmission of the Lamp*, "Huai-jang's Tao-i was like Hsing-ssu's Hsi-ch'ien: they were of the same source, but different streams; thenceforth the flourishing of the Ch'an teaching began with these two masters." Shih-t'ou and Ma-tsu, as they were usually known, produced a total of one hundred and sixty heirs to the teaching; it was common for dedicated students to call on both masters in their day, and several people were known to have succeeded to both Ma-tsu and Shih-t'ou. It was Ma-tsu who was the teacher of Pai-chang Huai-hai.

Huai-jang had been ordained and studied monastic discipline at Yu-ch'uan monastery in Hupei, an ancient center of T'ien-t'ai Buddhism. Huai-jang later gave up the study of precepts and aspired to Ch'an; he first called on Hui-an, one of the fifth patriarch's foremost heirs, then went south to see the sixth patriarch Hui-neng. After eight years with Hui-neng, Huai-jang was suddenly awakened, and stayed for another seven years delving into the innermost secrets of Ch'an. In 713 he went to Mt. Heng in Hunan, the southernmost of the five holy mountains in China, also known as Nan-yueh (whence Huai-jang's epithet). This also had been a center of T'ien-t'ai Buddhism. A small following seems to have gathered around Huai-jang, and he had six accomplished disciples, among whom Ma-tsu alone is said to have realized his "heart."

Sayings and Doings of Pai-chang

Ma-tsu and Huai-jang met on Nan-yueh during the 730's; at that time Ma-tsu was staying in a temple there constantly sitting in meditation. Huai-jang taught Ma-tsu what he called formless concentration, enabling him to transcend his sense of striving and attainment, to completely open his mind. Subsequently Ma-tsu stayed with Huai-jang for ten more years deepening his realization before he appeared in the world as a teacher on his own. Ma-tsu became one of the greatest Ch'an teachers of all time; legend has it that his appearance in the world was predicted by the Indian patriarch Prajnatara as part of the prophecy given to Bodhidharma before the latter came to China.

As in the case of the sixth patriarch and many other great Ch'an teachers, little is known of many of Ma-tsu's enlightened disciples, though a considerable portion of his recorded sayings are to be found in his dialogues with his students. Among Ma-tsu's many successors, it was Pai-chang Huai-hai whose teaching line flourished most and continued longest. Pai-chang's community of students is said to have numbered as many as one thousand people, and over a period of more than forty years of teaching he had thirty enlightened disciples; from his direct heirs came the founders of the famous Lin-chi and Kuei-Yang teaching lines, which figured prominently in the so-called golden age of Ch'an. Finally, as the founder of the unique Ch'an monastic system, he made a lasting contribution to Ch'an history and Chinese civilization which resounded throughout East Asia.

RECORD OF SAYINGS OF THE MEDITATION MASTER OF GREAT WISDOM (WHO LIVED ON) PAI-CHANG MOUNTAIN IN HUNG-CHOU

The master's initiatory name was Huai-hai, "Ocean of Heart", he was from Chang-le in Fukien, and his original surname was Wang. As a youth he left the dusts of the world and cultivated discipline, meditation, and wisdom, the three studies of Buddhism.[1] Finding Ta-chi (Ma-tsu, "Ancestor Ma")[2] teaching in Kiangsi province, he followed him in all sincerity. Along with Chih-tsang of Hsi-t'ang[3] and P'u-yuan of Nan-ch'uan[4] he was known as among those who "entered the room"; these three great heroes stood out like a tripod among them all.[5]

One day as the master was walking along with Ma-tsu, they saw a flock of wild ducks fly by. The ancestor said, "What is that?" The master said, "Wild ducks." Ma-tsu said, "Where have they gone?" The master said, "Flown away." Ma-tsu then turned around and grabbed the master's nose; feeling pain, the master let out a cry. The ancestor said, "Still you say, 'Flown away'?" At these words the master had insight.[6]

Then the master returned to the attendants' quarters, wailing pitifully. Another monk who worked as an attendant for Ma-tsu asked him, "Are you thinking of your parents?" The master said no. The fellow attendant said, "Has someone reviled you?" The master said no. The attendant said, "Then why are you crying?" The master said, "My nose was grabbed by the great teacher, and the pain hasn't stopped." The attendant said, "What happened? What didn't you realize?"[7] The master said, "Go ask the teacher."

The attendant went and asked the great teacher Ma-tsu, "What incident happened that attendant Huai-hai failed to accord with? He is in the attendants' quarters crying. Please explain this to me."

The great teacher, Ancestor Ma, explained simply that Huai-hai did indeed understand, and told the other attendant to go ask him. So the attendant went back and said to the master, "The teacher says you understand; he told me to ask you myself." The master then laughed. The attendant said, "Just a minute ago you were crying; now why are you laughing?"

The master said, "Just then I was crying; right now I am laughing."

The attendant was at a loss.

The next day Ma-tsu went into the teaching hall; as soon as the community had assembled, the master came forward and rolled up the prostration mat,[8] whereupon Ma-tsu got down from his seat and went back to his room with the master following behind.

Ma-tsu said, "Just then I had not yet said anything; why did you roll up the mat?" The master said, "Yesterday you grabbed my nose, and it hurt." Ma-tsu said, "Yesterday where did you set your mind?" The master said, "My nose doesn't hurt anymore today." Ma-tsu said, "You have deeply understood yesterday's event." The master bowed and withdrew.[9]

The master called on Ma-tsu a second time; as he stood by, Ma-tsu looked at the whisk on the corner of the rope seat. The master said, "Do you identify with the function, or detach from the function?" Ma-tsu said, "Later on, when you open your lips, what will you use to help people?" The master took the whisk and held it up; Ma-tsu said, "Do you identify with this function, or detach from this function?" The master hung the whisk back where it had been before; Ma-tsu drew himself up and shouted so loud that the master's ears were deafened for three days.[10]

Henceforth the sound of thunder would roll. Generous believers invited him to the region of Hsin-wu in Hung-chou, where he dwelt on Ta-hsiung Mountain.[11] Because of the precipitous steepness of the cliffs and crags where he dwelt, the mountain was called Pai-chang.[12] Once he was there, before even a month had passed, guests studying the mystery came like deer from all four directions; Kuei-shan[13] and Huang-po[14] were foremost among them.

When Huang-po came to the master's place, (after) one day[15] he took leave and said, "I want to go pay respects to Ancestor Ma." The master said, "Ancestor Ma has already passed on." Huang-po said, "What were Ancestor Ma's sayings?" The master then cited the circumstances of his second calling on Ancestor Ma and the raising of the whisk; he said, "The way of enlightenment is not a small matter; at that time, I was actually deafened for three days by Ma-tsu's shout."

When Huang-po heard this, he unconsciously stuck out his tongue (in awe). The master said, "Will you not succeed to Ma-tsu hereafter?" Huang-po said, "No. Today, thanks to your recital, I have been able to see Ancestor Ma's great capacity in action; but I do not know Ancestor Ma. If I were to succeed to Ancestor Ma, later on I would be bereft of descendants." The master said, "Right, right! When one's view is equal to the teacher's he diminishes his teacher's virtue by half; only when his view surpasses the teacher's is he qualified to pass on the transmission. You sure have a view that goes beyond a teacher's.[16]"

Later Kuei-shan asked Yang-shan,[17] "In the incident where Pai-chang called on Ancestor Ma a second time and raised the whisk, what was the essential meaning of those two venerable adepts?" Yang-shan said, "This is showing the function of great capacity." Kuei-shan said, "Ancestor Ma produced eighty-four enlightened teachers; how many people attained his great capacity, and how many attained his great function?" Yang-shan said, "Pai-chang attained the great capacity; Huang-po attained the great function. The rest were all just preachers of the Way." Kuei-shan said, "It is so."

Ma-tsu one day asked the master, "Where have you come from?" The master said, "From the other side of the mountain." Ma-tsu said, "And did you meet anyone?" The master said, "No." The ancestor said, "Why not?" The master said, "If I had, I would mention it to you." Ma-tsu said, "How could this be happening?" The master said, "I am at fault." Ma-tsu said, "On the contrary, it's my fault."

In the teaching hall the master said, "The spiritual light shines alone, far transcending the senses and their fields; the essential substance is exposed, real and eternal. It is not contained in written words. The nature of mind has no defilement; it is basically perfect and complete in itself. Just get rid of delusive attachments, and merge with realization of thusness."

Someone asked, "What is so extraordinary?" The master said, "Sitting alone on Ta-hsiung Mountain." The questioning monk bowed, whereupon the master hit him.[18]

Hsi-t'ang asked the master, "Later on, how will you open up and teach people?" The master closed and opened his hand twice. Hsi-t'ang said, "Then what?" The master tapped his head three times with his hand.

Ancestor Ma sent someone to take a letter and three jars of bean paste to give to the master. The master had him place them in the front of the teaching hall; then he went up into the hall. As soon as the community had gathered, he pointed at the bean paste jars with his staff and said, "If you can speak, I will not break them; if you cannot speak, then I'll break them." The community was speechless, so the master broke the jars and returned to his abbot's quarters.

A certain monk came crying into the teaching hall; the master said, "What are you doing?" The monk said, "My father and mother[19] have both died; please, Master, choose a day (for their funeral)." The master said, "Tomorrow bury them at once."

Someone asked, "What does it mean when 'to understand the meaning according to the scriptures is the enemy of the Buddhas of past, present, and future; to depart one word from the scriptures is the same as demon talk'?" The master said, "Steadfastly watching over activity and stillness is the enemy of the Buddhas of past, present, and future; to seek anything particular beyond this is the same as deluded demon talk."

Once when the Master had finished talking about the Way and the crowd was leaving the hall, he called to them; when the people turned their heads, he said, "What is it?"[20]

The master, having asked everyone to clear the fields, went back and asked Huang-po, "Reverend Yun, clearing fields is not easy." Huang-po said, "The community of monks is working." The master said, "There is strain on the work of the Way. Huang-po said, "How dare one avoid labor?" The master said, "How many fields have you cleared?" Huang-po made a gesture of hoeing the field, whereupon the master shouted; Huang-po covered his ears and went out.[21]

The master asked Huang-po, "Where have you come from?" Huang-po said, "From picking mushrooms on the mountain." The master said, "There is a tiger on the mountain; did you see him?" Huang-po immediately made a tiger's roar. The master took the axe at his side and made a gesture of chopping; Huang-po grabbed and held it, and immediately slapped the master.

In the evening, the master went up into the hall and said, "People, there is a tiger on the mountain; you people should all watch out for him coming and going. This morning I myself got bit by him."

Later Kuei-shan asked Yang-shan, "What about the story of Huang-po's tiger?" Yang-shan said, "What do you say, Teacher?" Kuei-shan said, "At that time Pai-chang should have immediately slain him with one blow of the axe; why should it come to this?" Yang-shan said, "I disagree." Kuei-shan said, "How do you see it?" Yang-shan said, "He not only rides the tiger's head, he also knows how to hold the tiger's tail." Kuei-shan said, "Chi, you sure have a dangerously precipitous statement there."

When the master went into the teaching hall each day, there was always an old man who listened to the teaching and then left as the assembly dispersed. One day he didn't leave, and the master asked him, "Who are you, standing there?"

The old man said, "In the time of the ancient Buddha Kasyapa, I used to dwell on this mountain. A student asked me, 'Is a highly cultivated and greatly accomplished person still subject to cause and effect?' I told him no, and I became subject to the body of a wild fox. Now I ask you, Teacher, is one greatly accomplished in practice still subject to cause and effect?"

The master said, "He is not ignorant of cause and effect." The old man was greatly enlightened at these words.

Bidding farewell to the master, he said, "I have already escaped the wild fox body; it lies on the other side of the mountain. I beg you to cremate it as you would a dead monk."

The master ordered the duty distributor to strike the gavel and announce to the monks that after the noon meal everyone was requested to assemble and see off a dead monk. The community couldn't understand this. The master led them to a cave on the other side of the mountain, and with his staff he dragged out a dead fox. Then he cremated it according to custom.

During the evening inquiry, after the master had recounted the preceding story, Huang-po asked, "A man of old gave a wrong answer and became subject to the body of a wild fox; today, if one makes no mistake time after time, then what?" The master said, "Come here and I'll tell you." Huang-po drew near and gave the master a slap; the master clapped his hands laughing and said, "I knew that barbarians' beards were red; here is another red-bearded barbarian."[22]

At that time Kuei-shan was in the community working as chief cook; the ascetic Ssu-ma[23] quoted the story of the wild fox to him and asked, "What about it, cook?" Kuei-shan rattled the door three times with his hands; Ssu-ma said, "Too coarse." Kuei-shan said, "The Buddhist teaching is not this principle."

Later, Kuei-shan quoted the story of Huang-po asking about the wild fox and asked Yang-shan about it. Yang-shan said, "Huang-po always uses this ability." Kuei-shan said, "Tell me, did he get it naturally, or did he get it from someone?" Yang-shan said, "It is both the inheritance of his teacher's bequest and his own communion with the source as well." Kuei-shan said, "So it is. So it is."

Huang-po asked, "What teaching did the ancients pass on to people since time immemorial?" The master was silent. Huang-po said, "How will descendants pass on the transmission in later generations?" The master said, "I thought you would be the one to do it," and then returned to the abbot's room.

As the master was doing chores along with Kuei-shan, he asked, "Is there any fire?" Kuei-shan said, "There is." The master said, "Where is it?" Kuei-shan picked up a piece of firewood, blew on it, and handed it over to the master. Taking it, the master said, "Like insects devouring wood."

In the course of hoeing the ground during general request to work, a certain monk, hearing the sound of the drum, lifted up his hoe and laughed aloud; then he went back to the monastery. The master said, "How excellent! This is the gate through which the sound seer enters into the principle."[24] Later he called the monk and asked him, "What truth did you perceive today?" The monk said, "Early this morning I didn't have any gruel; hearing the sound of the drum, I went back to eat rice." The master laughed.

Someone asked, "What is Buddha?" The master said, "What are you?" He said, "Me." The master said, "Do you know 'me' or not?" He said, "It's obvious." The master held up his whisk and asked, "Do you see the whisk?" He said, "Yes." The master then said no more.

The master sent a monk to Chang-ching,[25] saying, "When you see him go into the hall to talk about the teaching, spread your mat, bow, and rise; take one sandal, brush the dust off it with your sleeve, and put it back upside down."

When the monk got to Chang-ching, he did just as the master had instructed; Master Chang-ching said, "My fault."

As Kuei-shan, Wu-feng,[26] and Yun-yen were standing by, the master asked Kuei-shan, "With your mouth shut speak quickly!" Kuei-shan said, "I cannot speak. I ask you to speak, Teacher." The master said, "I do not decline to speak for you, but I'm afraid afterwards I would be bereft of descendants."

The master also asked Wu-feng the same thing; Wu-feng said, "You should shut up too, Teacher." The master said, "Where there is no one I shade my eyes to gaze far off at you."

He also asked Yun-yen; Yun-yen said, "I have something to say; please raise the question again, Teacher." The master said, "With your mouth shut, say it quickly!" Yun-yen said, "Do you now have (anything to say) or not, Teacher?" The master said, "I am bereft of descendants."

Going up into the teaching hall, he said to the assembly,"I want someone to take a message to Master Hsi-t'ang; who can go?"

Wu-feng said, "I can go."

The master said, "How will you transmit the message?" Wu-feng said, "I'll tell you when I return."

A monk asked Hsi-t'ang, "Where there are questions and answers, this I do not ask about now; what about when there are no questions or answers?" Hsi-t'ang said, "You fear decay, huh?"

When the master heard this quoted, he said, "Up till now I had doubted old brother Hsi-t'ang." Someone said,

"Please explain." The master said, "A compounded form cannot be grasped."

The master said to the assembly, "There is someone who never eats but doesn't say he's hungry; there is someone who eats all day but doesn't say he's full." No one had anything to say.

Yun-yen asked the master, "Everyday there's hard work; who do you do it all for?" The master said, "There is someone who requires it." Yun-yen said, "Why not have him do it himself?" The master said, "He has no tools."

When the master was a child, he went along with his mother into a temple to pay respects to the Buddha. He pointed to the statue and asked his mother, "Who is this?" His mother said, "He is a Buddha." The boy said, "His features are the same as a man's—later on I too shall be one."

When the master did chores he always was first in the community in taking up work. The people could not bear this so they hid his tools away early once and asked him to rest. The master said, "I have no virtue; how should I make others toil?" The master having looked all over for his tools without finding them, also neglected to eat. Therefore there came to be his saying that "a day without working is a day without eating," which circulated throughout the land.

The master died on the seventeenth day of the first month of the ninth year of the Yuan-he era of the T'ang dynasty (814); he was ninety-five years old. In the first year of Ch'ang-ch'ing (821), by imperial order he was entitled "Meditation Master of Great Knowledge." His memorial tower was called "Magnificent Jewel Disc."

Appendix to Record of Sayings

according to Ku-tsun-su yu-lu 1:

The master called on Great Teacher Ma and became his attendant. Every time a patron sent food for the meal, as soon as the master opened up the lid of the container, Great Teacher Ma would lift up a cake, show it to the assembly, and say, "What is this?" So it was every day. The master passed three years thus, when one day as he was walking along the road accompanying Patriarch Ma, he heard the call of wild ducks. Ma said, "What is that sound?" The master said "The call of wild ducks." After a pause, Ma said, "That call just then; where has it gone?" The master said,"Flown away." Patriarch Ma turned around and grabbed the master's nose and pulled it. The master made a cry of pain. Patriarch Ma said, "And you said, 'flown away'." At these words the master Pai-chang had insight.

Pai-chang's second calling on Ma-tsu is recorded as follows in the Ku-tsun-su yu-lu:

The master again called on Ma-tsu; the patriarch held up the whisk. The master said, "Do you identify with this function, or detach from this function?" After a long silence, Patriarch Ma said, "Hereafter when you open your lips, what will you use to help people?" The master then took the whisk and held it up; Ma-tsu said, "Do you identify with this function or are you detached from this function?" The master hung the whisk back in its former place; Ma-tsu thereupon shouted (so loud that) the master was deaf for three days.

EXTENSIVE RECORD OF PAI-CHANG

In language you must distinguish the esoteric and the exoteric;[1] you must distinguish generalizing and particularizing language, and you must distinguish the language of the complete teaching and the incomplete teaching.[2]

The complete teaching discusses purity; the incomplete teaching discusses impurity. Explaining the defilement in impure things is to weed out the profane; explaining the defilement in pure things is to weed out the holy.

Before the nine-part teaching[3] had been expounded, living beings had no eyes; it was necessary to depend on someone to refine them. If you are speaking to a deaf worldling, you should just teach him to leave home,[4] maintain discipline, practice meditation and develop wisdom. You should not speak this way to a worldling beyond measure, someone like Vimalakirti or the great hero Fu.[5]

Sayings and Doings of Pai-chang

If one is speaking to an ascetic,[6] the ascetic has already given his assent three times and his discipline is complete.[7] This is the power of discipline, concentration, and wisdom. To still speak in this way to him is called speaking at the wrong time, because the speech is not appropriate to the situation; it is also called suggestive talk.[8] To an ascetic one must explain the defilement in pure things—you should tell him to detach from all things, existent, nonexistent,[9] or whatever, to detach from all cultivation and experience, and even to detach from detachment.

While in the course of asceticism, one strips away influences of habit. If an ascetic cannot get rid of the diseases of greed and aversion, he too is called a deaf worldling; still he must be taught to practice meditation and cultivate wisdom.

As for monks of the two vehicles,[10] they have put an end to the disease of greed and aversion, removing them completely; they dwell in the absence of greed and consider that correct. This is the formless realm;[11] this is obstructing Buddha's light, this is shedding Buddha's blood.[12] You must teach them also to practice meditation and develop wisdom.

You must distinguish the terms of purity and impurity. "Impure things" have many names, such as greed, aversion, grasping love, etc. "Pure things" also have many names, such as enlightenment, extinction of suffering, liberation, etc. But while in the midst of the twin streams of purity and impurity, among such standards as profane and holy, amidst form, sound, smell, taste, touch, and phenomena, things of the world or things which transcend the world, the immediate mirror-like awareness should not have the slightest hair of grasping love for anything at all.

If one no longer loves or grasps, and yet abides in not loving or grasping and considers it correct, this is the elementary good;[13] this is abiding in the subdued mind. This is a disciple; he is one who is fond of the raft and will not give it up.[14] This is the way of the two vehicles. This is a result of meditation.

Once you do not grasp any more, and yet do not dwell in nonattachment either, this is the intermediate good. This is the half-word teaching.[15] This is still the formless realm; though you avoid falling into the way of the two vehicles, and avoid falling into the ways of demons,[16] this is still a meditation sickness.[17] This is the bondage of bodhisattvas.

Once you no longer dwell in nonattachment, and do not even make an understanding of not dwelling either, this is the final good; this is the full-word teaching. You avoid falling into the formless realm, avoid falling into meditation sickness, avoid falling into the way of bodhisattvas, and avoid falling into the state of the king of demons.

Because of barriers of knowledge,[18] barriers of station, and barriers of activity (practice), seeing one's own enlightened nature is like seeing color at night. As it is said, the station of Buddhahood cuts off twofold folly; the folly of subtle knowledge and the folly of extremely subtle knowledge.[19] Therefore it is said that a man of great wisdom smashes an atom to produce a volume of scripture.

If one can pass through these three phases,[20] one will not be constrained by the three stages. The doctrinal schools cite this and liken it to a deer leaping three times and getting out of the net. This is called an enlightened one beyond confinement—no thing can capture or bind him. He is one of the Buddhas succeeding to the Burning Lamp.[21] This is the supreme vehicle, the highest knowledge—this is standing on the way of enlightenment. This person is Buddha, and has the enlightened nature; he is a guide, able to employ the unobstructed wind.[22] This is unimpeded illumination.

After this, one will be able to freely use cause and effect, virtue and knowledge;[23] this is making a cart to carry cause and effect. In life one is not stayed by life; in death, one is not obstructed by death. Though within the clusters of matter, sensation, perception, coordination, and consciousness, it is as if a door had opened, and one is not obstructed by these five clusters. One is free to go or to stay, going out or entering in without difficulty. If you can be like this, there is no question of stages or steps, of superior or inferior; even down to the bodies of ants—if you can just be like this—all is the land of pure marvel. It is inconceivable.

This is still talk to untie bonds—"They themselves are whole; don't wound them!"[24] (Even) 'Buddha,' 'bodhisattva,' and such are wounds—as long as you speak of anything existent, nonexistent, or whatever, all these are wounds. 'Existence' and 'nonexistence' refer to all things.

(Even) those of the tenth stage[25] are (still) beings of the river of impure streams; they create a teaching of a pure stream, and establish characteristics of purity, explaining the afflictions of impurity.

In the past, the ten great disciples (of Shakyamuni Buddha)[26]—Shariputra, Purnamaitrayaniputra, Ananda of true faith, Sunakshatra of false faith, and the rest—each had his individual aspect, each had his individual characteristic condition. One by one they had their errors thoroughly explained away by the Guide. In the four stages of meditation and eight absorptions,[27] even saints and such dwell in absorption for as long as eighty thousand eons—they depend upon and cling to what they practice, intoxicated by the wine of pure things. Therefore people who are disciples, though they hear the teaching of the enlightened one, are not able to conceive the spirit of the unexcelled Way. That is why people who cut off the roots of goodness have no enlightened nature. A scripture says this is called the deep pit of liberation, a fearsome[28] place—if for one instant the mind retreats, it falls into hell as fast as an arrow shot.

Yet one cannot talk only in terms of retreating or of not retreating. Consider the likes of Manjusri, Avalokitesvara, and Mahasthamaprapta;[29] they come back to the stage of entering the stream (of the way to enlightenment),[30] mingling with various kinds of beings to lead them.[31] You cannot say that they retreat or regress; at such a time they are just called people who have entered the stream. If the immediate mirror awareness is just not concerned by anything at all, existent or nonexistent, and can pass through the three stages as well as through all things, pleasant or unpleasant, then even if one hears of a hundred, a thousand, ten thousand, or a hundred million Buddhas appearing in the world, it is just as if one had not heard; yet one does not dwell in not hearing either, nor does one make an understanding of not dwelling. You cannot say that this person retreats—measurements and calculations do not apply to such a one. This is "the Buddha always abiding in the world without being habituated to things of the world."

To say that the Buddha turns the wheel of the teaching and retreats (thereafter) is to slander the enlightened one, his teaching and community. To say that the Buddha does not turn the wheel of teaching and does not retreat is also to slander the enlightened one, the teaching and community. Seng-chao said, "The way of enlightenment cannot be measured or calculated—it is so high that there is nothing above it, so vast that it cannot be limited, so profound that it is bottomless, so deep that it cannot be fathomed. Speaking of it is like setting up a target mound inviting an arrow."[32]

To speak of the mirror awareness is still not really right; by way of the impure, discern the pure. If you say the immediate mirror awareness is correct, or that there is something else beyond the mirror awareness, this is all delusion.[33] If you keep dwelling in the immediate mirror awareness, this too is the same as delusion; it is called the mistake of naturalism.

To say the present mirror awareness is one's own Buddha is words of measurement, words of calculation—it is like the crying of a jackal. This is still being stuck as in glue at the gate. Originally you did not acknowledge that innate knowing and awareness are your own Buddha, and went running elsewhere to seek Buddha. So you needed a teacher to tell you about innate knowing and awareness as a medicine to cure this disease of hastily seeking outside. Once you no longer seek outwardly, the disease is cured and it is necessary to remove the medicine. If you cling fixedly to innate knowing awareness, this is a disease of meditation. Such is a thoroughgoing disciple; like water turned to ice, all the ice is water, but it can hardly be expected to quench thirst.

He also said,

With a fatal disease, ordinary physicians fold their arms, unable to do anything. There has never been such a thing as 'Buddha'—do not understand it as Buddha. 'Buddha' is a medicine for sentient beings. Without disease, one shouldn't take medicine. When medicine and disease are both dissolved, it is like pure water; Buddhahood is like a sweet herb mingling with the water, or like honey mixed with the water—it is most sweet and delicious. (But) if you judge from the standpoint of the pure water, it is not affected; it is not that it doesn't exist—it is originally there.

He also said,

This principle is originally present in everyone. All the Buddhas and bodhisattvas may be called people pointing out a jewel. Fundamentally it is not a thing—you don't need to know or understand it, you don't need to affirm or deny it. Just cut off dualism; cut off the supposition "it exists" and the supposition "it does not exist." Cut off the supposition "it is nonexistent" and the supposition "it is not nonexistent." When traces do not appear on either side, then neither lack nor sufficiency, neither profane nor holy, not light or dark. This is not having knowledge, yet not lacking knowledge, not bondage, not liberation. It is not any name or category at all. Why is this not true speech? How can you carve and polish emptiness to make an image of Buddha? How can you say that emptiness is blue, yellow, red, or white?

As it is said, "Reality has no comparison, because there is nothing to which it may be likened; the body or reality is not constructed and does not fall within the scope of any classification." That is why it is said, "The substance of the sage is nameless and cannot be spoken of; the empty door of truth as it really is cannot be tarried in." It is like the case of insects being able to alight anywhere, only they can't alight on the flames of a fire—sentient beings' minds are also like this in that they can form relations anywhere, only they cannot relate to transcendent wisdom.

When you call on teachers and seek some knowledge or understanding, this is the demon of teachers, because it gives rise to verbalization and opinion. If you rouse the four universal vows,[34] promising to rescue all living beings, only thereafter to finally attain Buddhahood yourself, this is the demon of the knowledge of the way of the warrior for enlightenment, because the vow is never given up. If you fast and control yourself, practice meditation and cultivate wisdom, these are afflicted roots of goodness.[35] Even if you sit on the site of enlightenment and manifest attainment of complete perfect awakening, and rescue innumerable people so that they all experience individual enlightenment, this is the demon of roots of goodness, since it arouses greedy attachment. If in the midst of all things you are utterly without any defilement by greed, so your aware essence exists alone, dwelling in exceedingly deep absorption, without ever rising or progressing anymore, this is the demon of concentration, because you'll be forever addicted to enjoying it, until ultimate extinction, detached from desire, quiescent and still. This is still demon work. If your wisdom cannot shed so many demon nets, then even if you can understand a hundred books of knowledge,[36] all of it is in the dregs of hell. If you seek to be like Buddha, there is no way for you to be so.

Now that you hear me say not to be attached to anything, whether good, bad, existent, nonexistent, or whatever, you immediately take that to be falling into emptiness. You don't know that to abandon the root and pursue the branches is to fall into emptiness; to seek Buddhahood, to seek enlightenment or anything at all, whether it may exist or not, this is abandoning the root and pursuing the branches.

For now, eat simple food to sustain life, patch rags to keep off the cold, when thirsty scoop up water to drink—beyond this, if one just harbors no thought at all of concern with anything at all, existent, nonexistent, or otherwise, this person will in time have his share of ease and clarity.

A good teacher does not cling to existence or nonexistence; he has abandoned the ten expressions of demon talk,[37] and when he speaks forth he does not entangle or bind others. Whatever he says, he does not call it a teacher's explanation; like a valley echo, "his words fill the land without fault."[38] He is worthy of trust and association.

If one should say, "I am capable of explaining, I am able to understand—I am the teacher, you are the disciple," this is the same as demon talk and is to speak of the Way pointlessly. Once you have actually seen the existence of the Way, (to say,) "This is Buddha, this is not Buddha, this is enlightenment, this is extinction, liberation," and so forth, is to pointlessly express partial knowledge, or lift a finger and say, "This is Ch'an! This is the path!" Such words entangle and bind others without end—this only increases the ties of mendicants. And even without speaking there is still fault of mouth. Rather be master of mind; don't be mastered by mind.

In the incomplete teaching there is a teacher of humans and gods (Buddha), there is a guide; in the complete teaching, he is not "teacher of humans and gods" and doesn't make doctrine the master. If you are not yet able to resort to the mystic mirror,[39] then for the time being, if you can resort to the complete teaching you will still have some share of familiarity with it. As for the incomplete teaching, it is only fitting to speak of it to deaf worldlings.

For now, just do not depend on anything existent, nonexistent, or whatever; and do not dwell in nondependence, and also do not make an understanding of not depending or dwelling. This is called great knowledge.

He also said,

Only a Buddha alone is a great teacher, because there is no second person; the rest are all called outsiders, also called demons talking.[40] Right now this is just to explain away dualism. Just do not be affected by greed for any existent or nonexistent things—when it comes to the matter of untying bonds, there are not special words or phrases to teach people. If you say that there are some particular verbal expressions to teach people, or that there is some particular doctrine to give people, this is called heresy and demon talk.

You must discern the words of the complete teaching and the incomplete teaching; you must discern prohibitive words and nonprohibitive words; you must discern living and dead words; you must discern medicine and disease words; you must discern words of negative and positive metaphor; you must discern generalizing and particularizing words.

To say that it is possible to attain Buddhahood by cultivation, that there is practice and there is realization, that this mind is enlightened, that the mind itself is identical to

Buddha—this is Buddha's teaching; these are words of the incomplete teaching. These are nonprohibitive words, generalizing words, words of a pound or ounce burden.[41] These are words concerned with weeding out impure things; these are words of positive metaphor. These are dead words. These are words for ordinary people.

To say that one cannot attain Buddhahood by cultivation, that there is no cultivation, no realization, it is not mind, not Buddha—this is also Buddha's teaching; these are words of the complete teaching, prohibitive words, particularizing words, words of a hundred hundredweight burden. These are words beyond the three vehicles' teachings, words of negative metaphor or instruction, words concerned with weeding out pure things; these are words for someone of station in the Way, these are living words.

From entering the stream all the way up to the tenth and highest stage of bodhisattvahood, as long as there are verbal formulations, all belong to the defilement of the dust of the teachings.[42] As long as there are verbal formulations, all are contained in the realm of affliction and trouble. As long as there are verbal formulations, all belong to the incomplete teaching.

The complete teaching is obedience, the incomplete teaching is transgression—at the stage of Buddhahood there is neither obedience nor transgression, as neither the complete nor the incomplete teachings are admissible.

From the sprouts discern the ground, from the impure discern the pure. Just be aware, mirrorlike, right now; if you assess the mirror awareness from the standpoint of purity, it is not pure, but absence of mirroring awareness is not pure either, neither is it impure. Nor is it holy or not holy. Also it is not seeing the impurity of the water and speaking of the ills of the water's impurity. If the water were pure, nothing could be said; speech instead would defile that water.

If there is a questionless question, there is also speechless speech. A Buddha does not explain the truth for the sake of Buddhas; in the equanimous, truly-so world of reality there is no Buddha—it doesn't save living beings. A Buddha does not remain in Buddhahood; this is called the real field of blessings.[43]

You must distinguish host and guest words.[44] If you are affected by greed for any existent or nonexistent objects, you are confused and disturbed by all existent or nonexistent objects. Your own mind then becomes the king of demons and its shining function belongs to the masses of deluding demons. If your present mirror awareness just does not dwell on anything, whatever may exist or not, mundane or transcendent, and also does not make an understanding of nondwelling, and also does not dwell in the absence of understanding, then your own mind is enlightened, Buddha, and its shining function belongs to the bodhisattvas—master of all mental conditions, its shining function is in the realm of passing phenomena. It is like waves telling of water; it illumines myriad forms without effort. If you can shine quiescently, then you will penetrate not only the hidden essence, but naturally past and present as well. As it is said, "When the spirit has no power to shine, the ultimate power always remains, able to be a guide in all places."[45]

The natural consciousness of sentient beings is of sticky and viscous nature because they have not yet tread the steps to enlightenment; for a long time they have stuck fast to various existent and nonexistent things. While they are partaking of the mystic essence, they cannot use it as medicine; while hearing words beyond conception, they cannot believe completely. That is why Shakyamuni, Gautama Buddha, spent forty-nine days under the tree of enlightenment silently contemplating. Wisdom is obscure, difficult to explain; there is nothing to which it may be likened. To say that sentient beings have enlightened nature is to slander the enlightened ones, their teachings and communities;[46] to say that sentient beings have no enlightened nature is also to slander the enlightened ones, their teachings and communities. If one says there is an enlightened nature, this is called slander by attachment, but to say there is no enlightened nature is called slander by falsehood. As it is said, to say that enlightened nature exists is slander by presumption, to say that it does not exist is slander by repudiation; to say that enlightened nature both exists and does not exist is slander by contradiction, and to say that enlightened nature is neither existent nor nonexistent is slander by meaningless argument. If a Buddha would not speak, then sentient beings would have no hope of liberation; if he would speak, then sentient beings would follow his words to produce interpretations—the benefits would be few and the disadvantages would be many. Therefore Buddha said, "I would rather not explain the truth, but enter extinction right away." But afterwards he thought back upon all the Buddhas of the past, who had all taught the doctrines of three vehicles.[47] Thereafter he made temporary use of verses to explain, and provisionally established names and terms. It is basically not Buddha, but to them he said, "This is Buddha;" it is originally not enlightenment, but he said to them, "This is enlightenment, peace, liberation," and so forth—he knew they couldn't bear up a hundred hundredweight burden, so for the time being he taught them the incomplete teaching. And he realized the spread of good ways, which was still better than evil ways—but when the limits of good results are fulfilled, then bad consequences arrive. Once you have "Buddha" then there are "sentient beings" there; once you have "nirvana," then there is "birth and death" there. Once you have light, then there is darkness there. As long as cause and effect with attachment are revolving over and over, there is nothing that does not incur a result.

If you want to avoid experiencing this reversal, just cut

off dualism; then measurements cannot govern you. You are neither Buddha nor sentient being, not near, not far, not high, not low, not equal, not even, not going, not coming; just do not cling to written letters which obstruct it,[48] and neither side (of any split) can hold you. You will avoid either form of pain or pleasure, and avoid the opposition of light and dark. The true principle is that even reality is not really real, and even falsehood is not false. It is not something calculable; like empty space, it cannot be cultivated. If there occurs any intellectual fabrication in the mind, then it is governed by measurements. This is also like the divination signs, which are governed by metal, wood, water, fire, and earth, or like sticky glue, stuck in five places—the king demon can grab you and freely return home.[49]

The words of the teachings all have three successive steps: the elementary, the intermediate, and the final good. At first it is just necessary to teach them to create a good state of mind. In the intermediate stage, they break through the good mind. The last is finally called really good—"A bodhisattva is not a bodhisattva; this is called a bodhisattva. The truth is not truth, yet is not other than truth."[50] Everything is like this. Yet if you teach only one stage, you will cause sentient beings to go to hell; if all three stages are taught at once, they will enter hell by themselves. This is not the business of a teacher.

Having explained as far as that the present mirror awareness is your own Buddha, this is the elementary good ("good in the beginning"). Not to keep dwelling in the immediate mirror awareness is the intermediate good ("good in the middle"). Furthermore not to make an understanding of nondwelling is the final good. As mentioned before, this is one of the Buddhas succeeding to the Burning Lamp; he is not an ordinary man nor a sage, but do not wrongly say a Buddha is neither an ordinary man nor a sage. The first patriarch in this country, Bodhidharma, said, "No ability, no sagacity—this is enlightened sagehood." But if you say Buddha is a sage, that is also wrong. The nine classes of spirits, dragons, beasts, and such species, from the gods Indra and Brahma on down, are all capable of transmutation, and the highest spirits also know the events of a hundred eons' time, past and present; but can they be Buddhas? Take the king of the titans for example; his body is immensely huge, comparable to two of Mount Everest, but when he did battle with Indra, king of gods, he knew his strength was not comparable, so he led his army of a million into the hole of a lotus root and hid there. His powers and abilities were not few, but he was not a Buddha.[51]

The gradations of the language of the teachings—haughty, relaxed, rising, falling—are not the same; what is called greed and aversion when one is not yet enlightened, not yet liberated, is called enlightened wisdom after enlightenment. That is why it is said, "He is not different from the man he was before; only his course of action is different from before."

Question: In cutting down plants, chopping wood, digging the earth and working the ground, do you think there will be any form of retribution for wrongdoing, or not?

The master said, One cannot definitely say there is wrongdoing, nor can one definitely say there is no wrongdoing. The matter of whether there is wrongdoing or not lies in the person concerned—if he is affected by greed for anything, whether it may exist or not, if he still has a grasping and rejecting mind, and has not passed through the three stages, this person can definitely be said to be doing wrong. If one passes beyond the three stages, inside the mind is empty, yet without making any conception of emptiness; this person can definitely be said to be blameless.

The master also said, If wrongdoing is committed and you say that you do not see that there is any wrongdoing, this too is not right at all. As it says in the vinaya, the fundamental illusion of killing, up to the point of the arousal aspect of killing,[52] still does not incur the wrongdoings of murder—how much less does the mind communicated in the Ch'an school incur any blame, being like in empty space, but not retaining a single action, yet without even an aspect of empty space—where could you attribute any wrongdoing?[53]

He also said, The way of meditation does not require cultivation; just do not be defiled.

He also said, Just melt the outer and inner mind together completely.

He also said, Just in terms of illumining objects, right now illumine all existing, nonexistent, or other things, utterly without any greedy clinging, and do not grasp.

He also said,

You should study like this: study is like washing a dirty garment—the garment is originally there, the dirt comes from outside. Having heard it said that all existent and nonexistent sound and form are such filth, do not set your mind on any of it at all. The thirty-two marks of greatness and eighty refinements under the tree of enlightenment[54] all belong to form, the twelve-branch teaching of the canon all belongs to sound—right now having cut off the flow of all existent and nonexistent sound and form, the mind will be like empty space. You should "study" in this way as urgently as saving your head afire; only then will you be capable of finding a road prepared already in the past upon which you can go when facing the end of your life. If you have not accomplished that yet, when you get to the moment of death and then try to compose yourself anew to start to learn, you have no hope of succeeding.

When facing the end, all are beautiful scenes appearing—according to what the mind likes, the most impressive are experienced first. If you do not do bad things right now, then at this time, facing death, there will be no unpleasant scenes. Even if there are any unpleasant scenes, they too will change into pleasant scenes. If you fear that at the moment of death you will go mad with terror and fail to attain freedom, then you should first be free right now—then you'll be all right.[55] Right now, in respect to each and every thing, don't have any loving attachment at all, and do not abide by intellectual understanding; then you will be free.

Right now is the cause; the moment of facing death is the result. When the resultant action is already manifest, how can you fear? Fear is over past and present; since the past had a present, the present must have a past. Since there has been enlightenment in the past, there must also be enlightenment in the present. If you can attain now and forever the single moment of present awareness, and this one moment of awareness is not governed by anything at all, whether existent, nonexistent, or whatever, then from past and present Buddha is just human, humans are just Buddhas. Also this is meditational concentration—don't use concentration to enter concentration, don't use meditation to conceive of meditation, don't use Buddha to search for Buddhahood. As it is said, "Reality does not seek reality, reality does not obtain reality, reality does not practice reality, reality does not see reality, but finds its way naturally." It is not attained by attainment; that is why bodhisattvas should thus be properly mindful, subsisting alone in the midst of things, composed, yet without knowledge of the fact of subsisting alone. The nature of wisdom is such as it is of itself; it is not disposed by causes. It is also called the knot of substance, also the cluster of substance.[56] It is not known by knowledge, not discerned by consciousness—it is entirely beyond mental calculation.

Frozen and silent, the body exhausted, thought and judgement are forever gone—like the flow of the ocean having ended, waves do not rise again.[57]

He also said,
Like the water of the ocean, without wind there are waves all around. Suddenly knowing of the waves all around being the gross with the subtle, letting go of knowledge in the midst of knowing is like the subtle within the subtle. This is the sphere of the enlightened ones, whence you really come to know; this is called the pinnacle of meditation, the king of meditation. It is also called knowledge of what is knowable, and produces all the various meditational states and anoints the foreheads of all princes of Dharma.[58] In all fields of form, sound, fragrance, flavor, feeling and phenomena, you realize complete, perfect enlightenment. Inside and outside are in complete communion, without any obstruction whatsoever.

One form, one atom, one Buddha, one form, all Buddhas, all forms, all atoms, all Buddhas—all forms, sounds, smells, feelings and phenomena are also like this, each filling all fields. This is the gross within the subtle, this is a good realm. This is the knowledge, discernment, seeing and hearing of all those in progress;[59] this is all those in progress going out in life and entering death, crossing over everything existent, nonexistent, whatever. This is what those in progress speak of, this is the nirvana of those in progress. This is the unexcelled Way, this is the spell which is peer to the peerless.[60]

This is the foremost teaching, and is considered the most exceedingly profound of all teachings; no human being can reach it, but all enlightened ones keep it in meditation,[61] like pure waves able to speak of the purity and defilement of all waters, their deep flow and expansive function. All enlightened ones keep this in mind—if you can be like this all the time, walking, standing, sitting or lying down, then will be revealed to you the body of pure clear light.

He also said,

As you are inherently equal, your words are equal, and I am also the same—a Buddha field of sound, a Buddha field of smell, a Buddha field of taste, a Buddha field of feeling, a Buddha field of phenomena—all are thus.[62] From here all the way to the world of the lotus treasury,[63] up and across, all is thus. If you hold onto the elementary knowledge as your understanding, this is called bondage at the pinnacle, and it is also called falling into bondage at the pinnacle.[64] This is the basis of all mundane troubles— giving rise to knowledge and opinion on your own, you "bind yourself without rope."

In terms of objects of knowledge, there are twenty-five states of existence[65] which bind the worlds; scattered through the avenues of the afflictions, you become entangled in them. This is elementary knowledge; the two vehicles see this and call it knowledge of what can be known, and they also call it subtle affliction; so they cut it off, and when it has been removed completely, this is called "returning the aware essence to the empty cave." It is also called intoxication by the wine of trance, and it is called the delusion of liberation. The world which is bound becomes and decays, but that which the power of concentration holds will leak out to another land, totally unawares. This is also called the deep pit of liberation, a place to be feared; bodhisattvas all stay far away from it.

In reading scriptures and studying the doctrines, you should turn all words right around and apply them to yourself. But all verbal teachings only point to the inherent nature of the present mirror awareness—as long as this is not affected by any existent or nonexistent objects at all, it is your guide; it can shine through all various existent and nonexistent realms. This is adamantine wisdom, where you have your share of freedom and independence. If you cannot understand in this way, then even if you could recite the whole canon and all its branches of knowledge, it would only make you conceited, and conversely shows contempt for Buddha—it is not true practice.

Just detach from all sound and form, and do not dwell in detachment, and do not dwell in intellectual understanding—this is practice. As for reading scriptures and studying the doctrines, according to worldly convention it is a good thing, but if assessed from the standpoint of one who is aware of the inner truth, this (reading and study) chokes people up. Even people of the tenth stage cannot escape completely, and flow into the river of birth and death.

But the teachings of the three vehicles all cure diseases such as greed and hatred. Right now, thought after thought, if you have such sicknesses as greed or hatred, you should first cure them—don't seek intellectual understanding of meanings and expressions. Understanding is in the province of desire, and desire turns into disease. Right now just detach from all things, existent or nonexistent, and even detach from detachment. Having passed beyond these three phases, you will naturally be no different from a Buddha. Since you yourself are Buddha, why worry that the Buddha will not know how to talk? Just beware of not being Buddha.

As long as you are bound by various existent or nonexistent things, you can't be free. This is because before the inner truth is firmly established, you first have virtue and knowledge; you are ridden by virtue and knowledge, like the menial employing the noble. It is not as good as first settling the inner truth and then afterwards having virtue and knowledge—then if you need virtue and knowledge, as the occasion appears you will be able to take gold and make it into earth, take earth and make it into gold, change sea water into buttermilk, smash Mount

Everest into fine dust, and pick up the waters of the four great oceans and put them into a single hair pore. Within one meaning you create unlimited meanings, and within unlimited meanings you make one meaning.

He also said,
If you lose your footing and become a wheel-turning king,[66] and have everyone in the world practice the ten virtues[67] for one day, this virtue and knowledge still cannot compare to your own mirror awareness; this is called the opportunity of kingship. When thoughts attach to various existent or nonexistent things, it is called the wheel-turning king. But right now, do not let any existent, nonexistent, or anything at all into your guts—go away beyond the four possibilities of logic. This is called emptiness, and emptiness is called the elixir of immortality, although we say that the elixir of immortality is taken along with the king, yet they are not two things, nor are they one thing. If you make interpretations of one or two, you are also called a wheel-turning king.

But right now suppose here is someone with virtue and knowledge who offered the necessities of life[68] to all kinds of beings[69] in four hundred trillion infinities of worlds, satisfying them according to their desires for eighty years; then he forms this thought: "Since these sentient beings are already deteriorating with age, I should teach them and guide them in the way to enlightenment, let them attain to the realization of entering the stream of the Way, on to the path of sainthood." Such a donor, just in giving sentient beings all means of comfort, already has immeasurable merit—how much the more if he caused them to attain the fruit of entering the stream, on to the path of sainthood; this merit is immeasurable, boundless, yet it is not comparable to the merit of the "fiftieth person hearing the scripture and rejoicing in accord."[70]

The *Scripture on Requiting Debt* says, "Lady Maya[71] gave birth to five hundred princes, who all attained self-enlightenment, and all became extinct—for each she set up a monument, made offerings, and bowed to them one by one. Sighing, she said, 'This is not as good as to have given birth to a single child who would have realized unexcelled enlightenment and saved me mental energy.' "

Right now, if there is one who attains, his worth is equal to a universe. That is why I always urge everyone to unlock the depths of inherent reality; if the truth within you is profound, you can use virtue and knowledge like a noble employing menials. It is also like a cart which does not stop. If you hold this as your understanding, this is called the jewel in the topknot; it is also called a jewel which has a price, and it is also called carrying excrement. If you do not hold to this as your understanding, this is like the king giving away the bright jewel in his topknot;[72] it is also called a great priceless jewel, and it is also called getting rid of excrement.[73]

A Buddha is just someone outside of bondage who comes back inside of bondage to be a Buddha in this way; he is someone beyond birth and death, just someone on the other side of mystic annihilation, but comes back to this shore to act thus as a Buddha. Neither humans nor apes can practice this. "Human" symbolizes the bodhisattvas of the highest, tenth stage; "ape" symbolizes ordinary people.

Reading the scriptures, studying the teachings, seeking all knowledge and understanding are not to be completely forbidden, but even if you can understand the teachings of the three vehicles, skillfully obtain pearl necklaces of adornment and get the cave of the thirty-two marks of greatness, if you seek Buddhahood you won't find it.[74]

The teachings say that even those students who greedily cling to the canon of the lesser vehicle should not be approached, let alone self-accredited immoral monks and nominal saints. In the *Scripture of the Great Decease* they are categorized among the sixteen wrong modes of behavior, the same as hunters and fisherfolk who purposely kill for profit.

The universally equal branch of the great vehicle teachings[75] is like ambrosia; it is also like poison—if you can digest it, it is like ambrosia, but if you can't digest it, it is like poison. In reading scriptures and studying the teachings, if you do not understand their living and dead words, you will certainly not penetrate the meanings and expressions therein. Then in that case, not to read is best.

He also said,

You should study the teachings, and you should also call on good teachers; foremost of all, you must have eyes yourself. You must discriminate those living and dead words before you can understand (scriptures and teachers); if you cannot discern clearly, you will certainly not penetrate them—this just adds to monks' bonds. That is why in teaching them to study the mystic essence, people are not made to read written letters. As it is said, speak of substance, do not speak of form; speak of meaning, not of wording—speaking like this is called true speech.

If you talk about the written letters, all of this is slander; this is called false speech. If bodhisattvas speak, they should speak according to the truth; this is also called true speech; they should make sentient beings hold to the heart, not hold to things, hold to practice, not hold to doctrine, speak of the person, not speak of the letter, speak of cultivation, not of literary embellishment.

"There is no meditation in the realm of desire" are also words of someone with one eye. Once it is said that there is no meditation in the realm of desire, how could one reach the realm of form? First, on the causal ground one cultivates two kinds of mental focus, after which one is able to reach the first meditation—focus with mental images and focus without mental images. Focus with mental images produces the realm of forms and such heavenly states as the four meditation heavens. Focus without mental images produces the formless realm and such heavenly states as the four empty realms. In the realm of desire clearly there is no meditation (ch'an); meditation begins in the realm of form.[76]

Question: How is it that now they say there is meditation (ch'an) in this land?
The master said,
Unmoved, not meditating, this is the meditation of those who come to realize thusness; it has nothing to do with producing meditational perceptions.[77]

Question: How is it that "sentient beings have no enlightened nature, but insentient beings have enlightened nature"?
The master said,
From humanity to Buddhahood is the grasping of holy sentiments; from humanity to hell is the grasping of ordinary sentiments. Right now as long as you have any mind of attached love in either realm, holy or ordinary, this is what is called sentient beings without enlightened nature. Right now if you have no grasping or rejecting mind for either realm, holy or ordinary, or for anything existent or nonexistent, and you have no awareness of not grasping or rejecting, this is called insentient being having enlightened nature. It's just that there are no emotional bonds, that's why it's called "insentient"—it's not the same as the insentience of wood or stone or space, of yellow flowers or green bamboo or considering these to possess enlightened nature. If you say that they have it, why do we not read in the scriptures of any one of them that received a

prophecy and attained Buddhahood? But the present mirror awareness, as long as it is not changed by having feelings, may be likened to green bamboo which never fails to conform with the situation; never failing to be aware of the time, it is likened to yellow flowers.

He also said,
If they tread the steps to Buddhahood, the insentient have enlightened nature; as long as they have not tread the steps to Buddhahood the sentient have no enlightened nature.

Question: How is it that the Buddha who was Victorious by Great Superknowledge sat on the site of enlightenment for ten aeons, but the attributes of Buddhahood did not become manifest in him and he could not fulfill the way of enlightenment?[78]
The master said,
"Aeon" means lingering, and it also means dwelling—dwelling in one virtue, lingering in ten virtues. What is called Buddha in India is called enlightened here. When their own mirror awareness lingers attached to goodness, those with faculties for goodness have no enlightened nature—that is why it is said that the attribute of Buddhahood didn't appear and he would not fulfill the way of enlightenment.

To dwell on evil when encountering evil is called the enlightenment of sentient beings; to dwell on goodness when encountering goodness is called the enlightenment of Buddhist disciples. Not dwelling on either side, good or bad, yet not making nondwelling an understanding, is called the enlightenment of bodhisattvas. Only neither dwelling nor making an understanding of nondwelling can finally be called the enlightenment of the Buddhas. As it is said, a Buddha does not dwell in Buddhahood; this is the real field of blessings.

If there is one in a million who attains this, he is called a priceless jewel, able to be a guide in all places—where there is no Buddha, he says, "This is Buddha," where there is no truth he says, "This is the true teaching," and where there is no community he says, "This is the community." This is called turning the great wheel of Dharma.

Question: Since high antiquity the ancestral schools have all had esoteric sayings handed down successor to successor; what about it?
The master said,
There are no secret sayings; those who come to realize thusness do not have a secret treasure. In the present mirror awareness, speech is distinctly clear; but if you seek formal characteristics, ultimately they cannot be found. This is an "esoteric saying."

From the stage of entering the stream up to the tenth stage of bodhisattvahood, as long as there are verbal formulations, all belong to the defilement of doctrine; as long as there are verbal formulations, all are contained within the realm of affliction; as long as there are verbal formulations, all belong to the incomplete teaching. As long as there are verbal formulations, all are impermissible. Even the complete teaching is wrong—what further esoteric saying do you seek?

Question: What is the meaning of the saying in the *Surangama Scripture*, "Space is born within great awareness, like a bubble from the ocean"?
The master said,
Space is symbolized by the bubble; the ocean is likened to nature. The nature of inherent, radiant awareness is greater than empty space, and therefore it is said that space is born within great awareness like a bubble from the ocean.

Question: What does it mean that one should "chop down the forest, not chop down the tree?"
The master said,
> The forest symbolizes mind; the tree symbolizes body. Because of talk about the forest, fear is aroused; therefore it is said, "Chop down the forest, don't chop down the tree."

Question: Seng-chao said that "words are like a target mound inviting an arrow"—since talk is like a target, it is impossible to avoid injury. Since the trouble involved is the same, how can the adept and the naive be distinguished?
The master said,
> Just shoot back an arrow to stop the other on the way; if they (the arrows) miss each other, there is bound to be some injury sustained. If you seek echoes in a valley, they are forever formless; the echo is in the mouth, gain and loss is in the coming question. If you then ask what it goes back to, instead you get hit by an arrow. It's also like, "If you know the illusion, it's not illusion." The third patriarch of Ch'an said, "If you don't know the hidden essence, you'll uselessly work at concentrating on stillness."
>
> If you recognize things and consider that seeing, this is like holding tiles and pebbles; what do you want to hold on to them for? If you say you don't see, then how are you different from wood or stone? That is why seeing and not seeing both have their fault. I have quoted an example of that.

Question: How is it that "there are originally no afflictions, nor the thirty-two marks of greatness"?
The master said,
> This is a matter pertaining to Buddhahood. Originally there were afflictions, now there are the thirty-two marks of greatness; the ordinary state of mind at present is what these are.

Question: How is it that a bodhisattva with a boundless body does not see the mark on the Buddha's forehead?[79] The master said,

Because he entertains views of bounds and boundlessness, therefore he does not see the mark on Buddha's forehead. Right now if you have no views such as of existence, and also have no views of nothingness, this is called the appearance of the mark on the forehead.

Question: Nowadays monks all say, "We follow the Buddhist teaching, and study a scripture, a treatise, a meditation, a rule, a knowledge, an understanding—we should receive the offerings of the four necessities of life from patrons." Do you think they can digest the offerings? The master said,

Just going by the present shining function, in each sound, form, fragrance and taste, in the midst of all various existent and nonexistent things, in every realm, if one has not the slightest spot of grasping indulgence, and yet does not abide in nongrasping, and does not even have any understanding of nonabiding, this person can eat ten thousand ounces of gold's worth and still be able to digest it.

But right now as you shine on all things existent, nonexistent, etc., even if you cut off accretions in the gates of the senses, if there is the slightest hair of greedy love remaining unconquered, then if you beg even a single grain of rice or a single thread of cloth from a patron, for each you will wear fur and horns, pull plows and bear burdens; one by one you must repay him before you can say you don't depend on Buddha.

A Buddha is someone with no attachments, someone with no seeking, someone without resort—now if you longingly search for Buddha here and there, then you have totally turned away from him. Therefore it is said, "Though long having been closely associated with Bud-

Sayings and Doings of Pai-chang

dha, they do not know the enlightened nature." For those who only look at the saviour of the world, to say that one sees Buddha only after evolving in the six dispositions for a long time[80] is in order to explain that a Buddha is hard to meet. Manjusri is the ancestral teacher of the seven Buddhas of antiquity.[81]

Manjusri is the principal, leading bodhisattva of this world, yet because he pointlessly created the idea of seeing Buddha and the idea of hearing the Dharma, he was overcome by the Buddha's inconceivable power and cast down between the two iron enclosing mountains.[82] It is not that he does not know how to specially act as a standard for students; he is commanding all students of later times not to create such seeing and hearing. Just have no doctrines of existence, nonexistence, etc., no views of existence, nonexistence, etc.—one by one pass through and beyond the three states. This is called the wish-fulfilling jewel;[83] this is called jewel flowers supporting your feet.[84]

If you create a view of Buddha or a view of Dharma, or views of anything at all, existent, nonexistent, or whatever, these are called the (illusory) visions of the eye-diseased; because of what is seen, they are also called the enclosure of views, the lid of views, and also the affliction of views.

Right now, in moment after moment of awareness, if all seeing, hearing, discerning and knowing, and all defiling dusts of afflictions and passions are thoroughly cleared away, then even be it one atom, one form, always it is one Buddha; even one moment of thought is always the past, present, and future five clusters of life elements of one Buddha. Thought after thought—who knows how many—this is what is called Buddhas filling empty space; this is called the Buddha dividing his body;[85] this is called the precious shrine appearing.[86]

Therefore I always sadly say that, as we see the life we depend on today, it depends on a grain of rice, a blade of vegetable to eat—if we do not get food from time to time we starve, if we do not get water we die of thirst, and if we do not have fire we freeze to death. If we lack for one day we don't live, yet if we lack for one day we don't die either—we are in the grip of the gross elements. This is not as good as our predecessors, who entered fire without being burnt, entered water without drowning;[87] yet if they wanted to burn, they burnt, and if they wanted to drown, they drowned. When they wanted to live, they lived, and when they wanted to die they died—they were free to go or stay. Such people have their share of freedom; if the mind is not disturbed, there is no need to seek Buddha, to seek enlightenment or extinction from suffering. If you seek with attachment to Buddha, you are in the province of greed, and greed turns into disease. Therefore it is said, "The Buddha disease is most difficult to cure; only by slandering the Buddha and reviling the Dharma can you take food."[88] "Food" means your own purely aware essence—the meal of non-indulgence, the food of liberation; these words cure the illness of the bodhisattvas of the tenth stage. From the first to the tenth stage of bodhisattvahood they are still disciples—right now as long as they have any seeking mind at all, they're all called immoral monks, nominal saints; they're all called jackals.[89] Clearly they can't digest the offerings of others.

But right now if one hears sound as an echo, smells odor as wind, detached from all existent, nonexistent, or any things at all, and yet does not dwell in detachment, and has no understanding of not dwelling either, this person cannot be affected by any moral defilement.

For one to be called renunciant because of the search for unsurpassed enlightenment and ultimate peace is still a false aspiration—how much the more so is worldly disputation, seeking victory and defeat, saying "I am able, I understand," seeking a following, liking a disciple, being fond of a dwelling place, making a pact with a patron (for) a robe, a meal, a name, a gain; and they say, "I have attained total unimpeded freedom." They are only fooling themselves.

Right now if you are capable, within your own five clusters of mortal being, of not acting as the owner—though cut to pieces joint by joint by others, yet not having any thought of resentment or regret, and also not suffering, and so on, even when your own disciples are beaten head to foot by others—in each case of events such as these, if you do not have even a single thought giving rise to ideas of others and self, yet abide in the absence of even a single thought and consider that right, this is called defilement by the dust of the Dharma.[90] Even people in the tenth stage of bodhisattvahood cannot get rid of this completely, and flow into the river of birth and death. This is why I always urge everyone to fear the affliction by the dust of Dharma as you would fear the states of hell beings, hungry ghosts, and animals—then you will have a share of independence. If one surpassed nirvana, if he did not arouse the slightest notion of marvel or esteem therefore, this person, step after step, would be a Buddha;[91] he does not need for his feet to tread upon lotus flowers or to divide his body into a hundred million. But right now, if you have the slightest bit of love for anything existent or nonexistent defiling your mind, then even if your feet did tread upon lotus flowers, it would still be the same as demon's work.

If one clings to "original purity, fundamental liberation" and considers himself a Buddha, considers his own self to be Ch'an and the Way, then he belongs to the naturalist outsiders. If one clings to causality, the perfection of practice and attainment of realization, then he belongs to the outsiders who believe in causality. If you cling to existence, then you belong to outsiders with the notion of eternity; if you cling to nonexistence, you belong to outsiders with the notion of annihilation. If you cling to both existence and nonexistence, then you belong to outsiders with extreme views. If you cling to neither existence nor nonexistence, then you belong to outsiders with a notion of emptiness.

You ignorant, stupid outsiders, right now just do not create any views of Buddha or views of nirvana; when you have no views at all of existence, nonexistence, or whatever, and yet do not lack vision, this is called true vision. To have no hearing at all, yet not to lack hearing, is called true hearing. This is called smashing down outside ways. No bedevilments of the two vehicles befall—this is the "greatest enlightening charm." None of the bedevilment of bodhisattvas befalls—this is the "unexcelled charm." None of the bedevilment of Buddhas befalls—this is the "peerless charm."[92]

One transformation, into sentient beings from fawning, deceitful titans; second transformation, into members of the two vehicles from fawning, deceitful titans; third transformation, into bodhisattvas from fawning, deceitful titans. These are the three transformed pure lands.[93]

But all things, existent, nonexistent, ordinary, sacred, may be likened to gold ore; the self is like the veins of gold. When the gold and ore are separated, the real gold is exposed. If there is someone who is seeking money or treasure, you then turn the gold into money and give it to them. It's also like wheat flour, its substance pure, without any mineral salts; if someone wants cake, you turn the flour into cake and give it to them. It's also like a wise minister who skillfully interprets the meaning of the king—when the king is going to travel and asks for *saindhava*, then the minister brings a horse; at mealtime, when the king wants *saindhava* the minister serves salt.[94] These all symbolize people who study the hidden essence, who are skillfully able to communicate and respond to situations faultlessly. It's also called the six absolute lions.[95] Master Chi said, "There are a hundredfold differences in what is made, according to the person."[96]

Bodhisattvas of the tenth stage are not hungry, not satisfied; they enter water without drowning, enter fire without burning—yet if they want to burn, they cannot burn; they are governed by limitations. A Buddha is not like this—he enters fire without burning, but if he wants to burn, then he burns; if he wants to drown, he drowns. He is able to use the four elements, wind and water, freely.[97] "All forms are the form of Buddha, all voices are the voice of Buddha"; when your own defiled, hypocritical, devious mind is exhausted completely, and you pass beyond the three states, you will be able to say such words.[98]

The pure disciples of bodhisattvas are lucid and clear; whatever they say, they do not cling to nonexistence or existence—all their awareness and activity is not contained by either purity or impurity.

He who has disease but does not take medicine is a fool. He who has no disease but takes medicine is someone who is a disciple; one who clings fixedly to the teaching is called a disciple of fixed nature. One wholly devoted to much learning is called a disciple who is conceited. Obviously these are what are called disciples with something yet to learn. Those sunk in emptiness, lingering in stillness and self-knowledge, are called disciples with nothing more to learn.[99]

Greed, anger, folly, and the like, are poisons; the Buddhist teachings are medicine. When the poison is not yet dispersed, the medicine should be removed. If you take medicine when you have no illness, the medicine turns into illness. When the disease is gone but the medicine is not dissipated, 'unborn and imperishable' then has the meaning of impermanence.[100]

The *Nirvana Scripture* says that there are three evil desires: one is the desire to be surrounded by monks, nuns, and men and women devotees, the second is the desire to have everybody as your own followers, the third is the desire to have everyone know you as a sage and saint. The

Kasyapa Scripture says that one evil desire is to obtain sight of the Buddhas of the future, a second is the desire to obtain world monarchy, a third is the desire to obtain a great name as a warrior, the fourth is the desire to obtain a great name as a priest. And so on, even to despising birth and death and seeking nirvana; such wrong desires as this must first be cut off. Right now, as long as you have grasping attachment and wandering thoughts, all are called wrong desires; all are in the realm of the six heavens of desire, all governed by the Evil One.[101]

Question: What is "constantly clearing away excrement for twenty years"?[102]

The Master said,

Just put to rest all knowledge and views of existence and nonexistence; just put an end to all greedy seeking—one by one pass through the three stages of liberation in respect to everything. This is called clearing away excrement.

But now if you seek Buddha, seek enlightenment, or seek anything, existent, nonexistent, or otherwise, this is called carrying excrement in, it is not called carrying excrement out. Now if you create an idea of Buddha, create an understanding of Buddha, as long as there is anything envisioned, anything sought, it's all called the excrement of fabricated conceptualizations. It's also called rough speech, and it is called dead words. As it is said, "The great ocean does not retain a dead corpse." Idle talk is not what is called fabricated conceptualizations; if the speaker discussed purity and impurity, that is called fabricated conceptualization. The written teachings contain twenty-one kinds of emptiness in all, to clear away the passions and afflictions of all sentient beings.

An ascetic maintains discipline of diet and behavior, is tolerant, gentle, compassionate, rejoices in abandonment. This has always been the norm for monks; once one has conformed in this way, clearly he is in accord with the Buddhist teaching—but one should not cling greedily or hold fast to it. If you long to attain Buddhahood, or to obtain such a thing as enlightenment, it is like your hand touching fire.[103]

Manjusri said, "If one creates ideas of Buddha or Dharma, that person will surely harm himself." For this reason Manjusri wielded a sword before Gautama, and Angulimalya brandished a knife against the Shakya.[104] As it is said, a bodhisattva commits the five acts which bring immediate uninterrupted retribution, yet does not enter uninterrupted hell—that is the uninterruption of mystical experience; it is not the same as the uninterrupted hell of those sentient beings who commit the five deadly crimes.[105]

From evil demons right up to Buddhas, all is defilement; when there is not a trace of dependent clinging anywhere, such is called the way of the two vehicles. How much less (should anyone cling to) disputation, looking for victory and defeat, saying, "I am able, I understand"—such are just argumentative monks, they are not to be called nonstriving monks.

For now just do not be influenced by greed for anything at all, existent or nonexistent; this is called birthlessness, and it is called true faith. To believe insistently in all things is called incomplete faith; it is also called imperfect faith, and it is called biased faith. Because faith is incomplete, one is called hopeless.

Now if you wish to be able to be immediately enlightened, just let person and things both disappear, person and things both be cut off, person and things both be empty—passing through beyond the three stages, this is called someone who doesn't fall within any categorizations. This is believing in Dharma; this is discipline and liberality, learning and wisdom, and so forth. Bodhisattvas are willing to forego fulfilling Buddhahood, are willing to forego being sentient beings, are willing to forego holding to discipline, are willing to forego violating discipline—therefore it is said that they neither obey nor transgress.

Knowledge is impure, illumination is pure; wisdom is pure, consciousness is impure. What in Buddhas is called illuminating wisdom is called knowledge in bodhisattvas; in the two vehicles and ordinary sentient beings it is called consciousness, and it is also called affliction. In Buddhas it is called speaking of cause from within the state of result; in sentient beings it is called speaking of result from within the state of cause. In Buddhas it is called turning the wheel of Dharma; in sentient beings it is called the wheel of Dharma turning. In bodhisattvas what is called precious adornments is called the thicket of the mortal cluster in sentient beings—in Buddhas it is called the original ground of ignorance; because this ignorance is itself illumination, therefore it is said that ignorance is the substance of the Way. It is not the same as the dark-enshrouded ignorance of sentient beings.

That is object, this is subject; that is heard, this is the hearer. "Not one, not different, not restricted, not eternal, not coming, not going"—these are living words; these are words which have gotten out of the rut—not light, not dark, not Buddha, not sentient being; all is like this. "Coming, going, annihilation, eternity, Buddha, sentient being"—these are dead words; "universal, non-universal, same, different, finite, eternal," and so forth, are all irrelevant theories. The transcendent wisdom is your own enlightened nature.

In *Mahayana*, *maha* means "great" and *yana* means "vehicle." If you hold fast to your own inherent knowing and awareness, you too will become a naturalist heretic. Do not remain in your immediate mirror awareness, but do not seek enlightenment elsewhere. If you still seek elsewhere in some special way, you subordinate yourself

Sayings and Doings of Pai-chang

to the heretics who believe in causality. The first patriarch in this country, Bodhidharma, said, "If the mind affirms something, it must deny something too." If you value a single thing, you are deluded by that thing; esteem anything and you are confused by it. Believe, and you are deluded by belief; disbelief still amounts to repudiation. Do not value, do not devalue; do not believe, do not disbelieve.

Buddhahood is also not inactivity; though it is not inactive, yet it is not dark quiescence. Like empty space, the Buddha is a great-bodied being with much reflective awareness; but although his reflective awareness is great, his awareness is pure and clear—the demons of greed and aversion cannot hold him. Buddha is someone beyond confinement; he has not a trace of lust or attachment, and yet has no knowledge of having no lust or attachment. This is known as fulfilling myriad practices through six ways of transcendence.[106] If he needs articles of adornment, he has all kinds; if he doesn't need them and doesn't use them, still he hasn't lost them. He can use virtue and knowledge as cause and effect freely. This is cultivation; it is not that taking on laborious works and shouldering a burden are what is called cultivation—on the contrary, it is not so.

The three bodies (of Buddha) are one substance; the single substance has three bodies. One is the body of reality, the real aspect of Buddha. The real aspect of Buddha is not bright, not dark—illumination and obscurity both are in the realm of illusion. The real aspect, or real character, gets its name from being contrasted to emptiness; orginally there were no names at all. As it is said, the Buddha Body is uncreated and does not fall within the scope of any categories.

Attaining Buddhahood, being offered a canopy,[107] etc., are words of a pound or ounce burden; the names derive from the need to distinguish the pure by means of the impure. Thus it is said that the body of reality in its genuine aspect is called Vairocana Buddha as the pure and clear reality body.[108] It is also called the empty reality-body Buddha, and it is called the great perfect mirror knowledge, and it is called the eighth consciousness.[109] It is also called the source of nature, and it is also called the empty source. It is called the Buddha dwelling in the land which is neither pure nor defiled. It is also called the lion in his den. It is also called adamantine applied knowledge, and it is called the spotless altar. It is also called the primary void, and it is called the hidden essence. The third patriarch of Ch'an said, "Without knowing the hidden essence, it is useless to work at concentration on stillness."

Secondly, the reward-body Buddha is the Buddha under the tree of enlightenment. This is also called the illusory transformation Buddha, and it is called the beatified Buddha. This is called Locana Buddha as the completely fulfilled body of reward.[110] It is also called the knowledge of the essential equality of things, and it is also called the seventh consciousness. It is also called the Buddha as responding result in accordance with cause. It is equal in all the fifty-two stages of meditation,[111] equal in saints and self-enlightened ones, equal in all bodhisattvas, and is equally subject to such pains as birth and death, but is not equally subject to the misery of sentient beings' binding activities.

Third is the manifestation-body Buddha. Now in the midst of all things, existent and nonexistent, when there is utterly no stain of longing, and there is no nonstaining, detached from four logical possibilities (of being, nonbeing, neither, both) such words and intelligence as there may be is called the manifestation-body Buddha. This is called Shakyamuni Buddha with a thousand hundred hundred thousand manifestation bodies. It is also called the great miraculous transformation, and it is called wandering at play in spiritual powers. It is also called the subtle analytic observation knowledge, and it is called the sixth consciousness.

To make offerings means to purify the threefold activity (of body, mouth, mind)—before, there is no affliction to cut off; in the meantime there is no inherent nature to be preserved; afterwards there is no Buddhahood to obtain. This is the three times cut off, threefold action being pure. This is the emptiness of the three spheres (of activity of body, mouth, and mind), and the emptiness of the three elements of giving (giver, receiver, gift).

How does a monk serve Buddha? That which is called the nonindulgent six senses is also called "adornments." Emptiness has no indulgence; forests and trees adorn it. Emptiness has no defilement; flowers and fruits adorn it. Emptiness has no Buddha eye; it depends on the reality eye of someone who cultivates it to distinguish the pure and defiled without any understanding that he is discriminating the pure and defiled—this is called "ultimately no eye."

In the *Ratnakuta Scripture* it says, "The body of reality cannot be sought by means of seeing, hearing, discernment or knowledge. It is not that which is seen by the physical eye, because it has no form. It is not that which is seen by the divine eye, because it has no falsehood. It is not that which is seen by the eye of wisdom, because it is outside of attributes. It is not that which is seen by the eye of objective reality, because it is beyond all activity and configuration. It is not that which is seen by the enlightened (Buddha) eye, because it is beyond all modes of consciousness." If one does not produce such views as these, this is called the view of Buddha. Same as matter, yet not matter; same as emptiness, yet not emptiness—this is what is called true emptiness. 'Matter' and 'emptiness' are also expressions of medicine and disease quelling each other. In the *Analysis of the Real Universe*, Tu-shun[112] says, "It is not proper to say either 'identical to matter' or 'not identical to matter.' And then again it is not proper to say either 'identical to voidness' or 'not identical to voidness.' "

When the eye, ear, nose, tongue, body, and mind do not admit anything existent or nonexistent, this is called evolving into the seventh stage. Bodhisattvas of the seventh stage do not fall back from the seventh stage; on the three stages above this, bodhisattvas' mind ground is clear and pure, easily stained; when speaking of fire, they are immediately burned.

Going upward from the realm of form, liberality is sickness and parsimony is medicine; going downward from the realm of form, parsimony is sickness and liberality is medicine.[113]

The discipline of doing is to cut off the things of the world. Just do not do anything yourself, and there is no fault—this is called the discipline of nondoing. It is also called unmanifested discipline, and it is also called the discipline of nonindulgence. As long as there is arousal of mind and movement of thoughts, this is all called breaking discipline.

For now just do not be confused and disturbed by any existent or non-existent objects; and do not stop and abide in disillusion, and yet have no understanding of nonabiding. This is called all-embracing study; this is called effort, praise, and remembrance, and it is called widespread circulation of truth.

When not yet enlightened, not yet liberated, it is called mother; after enlightenment, it is called child. When there is not even any knowledge or understanding of the absence of enlightenment or liberation, that is called "mother and child both perish." There is no confinement by good, no confinement by evil; no confinement by Buddha, no confinement by sentient beings. The same goes for all assessments or measurements, to the extent that there is no confinement by any calculating measurements at all. Therefore it is said that a Buddha is someone who has left confinement and goes beyond measure.

To be greedily fond of knowledge and understanding of meanings and expressions is like a mother loving her child—she only gives the child a lot of refined milk to drink, without knowing at all whether the child can digest it or not. These words describe the affliction of those on the tenth stage of bodhisattvahood receiving the honor of people and gods—producing the meditation states of the form and formless realms, the affliction of prosperity and happiness; not having attained free use of supernatural powers to fly aloft, concealing and revealing oneself, the affliction of going to all the pure lands of the Buddhas everywhere to listen to their teachings,[114] cultivating love, compassions, joy and equanimity, the affliction of the middle way; learning the three illuminations and six super-knowledges,[115] the affliction of the four aspects of unhindered intellect;[116] cultivating the mind of the great vehicle, the affliction of undertaking the four universal vows.[117]

The first, second, third, and fourth stages have the affliction of clear understanding; the fifth, sixth, and seventh stages have the affliction of various kinds of knowledge; the eighth, ninth, and tenth stages have the afflictions of bodhisattvas simultaneously illumining both realities,[118] on up to the affliction of cultivating the fruit of Buddhahood and its innumerable practices—you only care for knowledge and understanding of meanings and expressions, and don't realize that instead these are binding afflictions. Therefore it is said that the river of views can float a scent-bearing elephant.[119]

Question: (Do you) see or not?
The master said, (I) see.
Question: How is it after seeing?
The master said,
Seeing is nondual. Since I say seeing is nondual, one

does not see sight by means of sight. If you see upon seeing, is the prior seeing veritable, or is the latter seeing veritable? As it is said, when seeing seeing, seeing is not seeing. Since seeing is even apart from seeing, seeing cannot reach it. Therefore, if you do not exercise a way of seeing, do not exercise a way of hearing, and do not exercise a way of discernment, all the Buddhas will quickly give you a prediction of complete enlightenment.

Criticism: Since seeing is not giving prediction of enlightenment, what is the use of giving the prediction?
The master said,

People of the past who awakened to the source were not trammeled by anything existent or nonexistent, like having washed a dirty garment. Thus it is said that detachment from form is called Buddha. When falsehood and truth do not remain at all, the central essence is the solitary mystery; mystically arriving on a single road, later followers of the same path accord with that stage. Thus we speak of giving prediction, that's all.

Ignorance is father, greed is mother. Self is the disease, yet self is the medicine too. The self is a sword, and it kills one's own father and mother, ignorance and greed. Therefore I say you should kill your father and mother. One expression categorically smashes through all things. "Eating food at the wrong time" is also like this—right now, be it anything existent, nonexistent, whatever, all are "eating the wrong food." They're also called bad food. This is impure food placed in a precious vessel; this is breaking discipline, this is defiling the vessel, this is mixed (impure) food.

A Buddha is someone who does not seek; right now if you greedily seek anything, existent or nonexistent, whatever you have, whatever you do, all goes against (Buddhahood)—instead this is repudiating Buddha. As long as there is affection of greed, it's all called "giving the hands."

Right now, just do not be affected by greed; and do not abide in not being affected by greed, and yet have no understanding of nonabiding. This is called the fire of wisdom. This is burning the hands and fingers, this is not sparing bodily life, this is being dismembered joint by joint, this is leaving the world, this is lifting the world in another quarter in the palm of the hand.[120]

But right now, of the twelve branches of the canonical Buddhist teaching, or anything existent or nonexistent, if you have the slightest hair kept in your guts, you have not gotten out of the net. As long as there is something sought, something gained, as long as there is arousal of mind and stirring of thought, all are called jackals.

If within one's guts there is absolutely nothing sought, absolutely nothing gained, this person is a great donor. This is the lion's roar.[121] If one still doesn't dwell in nonpossession and also has no understanding of not dwelling, this is called the six absolute lions. When selfhood is not conceived, various evils do not arise—this is "putting Mount Everest into a mustard seed." Not arousing any greed, anger, or the eight winds or such,[122] is being able to sip all the waters of the four oceans into the mouth. Not accepting any false speech is not letting it into the ears. Not letting the body cause evil deeds toward others is containing all fire within the belly.

Right now, in regard to each object, not being confused, not disturbed, not angered, not joyful, removing the accretions in the gates of one's own six senses until they're purified, this is a person with no concern over anything. This surpasses all knowledge and understanding, asceticism and effort. This is called the divine eye. This is called the nature of the cosmos. This is making a cart to carry cause and effect.

When a Buddha appears in the world to rescue sentient beings, then the prior thought is not born; the succeeding thought should not be continued. When the activity of preceding thoughts vanishes, this is called rescuing sentient beings. If the preceding thought was angry, he uses the medicine of joy to cure it. Then it is said that there is a Buddha saving sentient beings.

However, all verbal teachings just cure disease; because the diseases are not the same, the medicines are also not the same. That is why sometimes it is said there is Buddha, and sometimes it is said there is no Buddha. True words cure sickness; if the cure manages to heal, then all are true words—if they can't effectively cure sickness, all are false words. True words are false words insofar as they give rise to views; false words are true words insofar as they cut off the delusions of sentient beings. Because disease is unreal, there is only unreal medicine to cure it.

(To say that) "the Buddha appears in the world and saves sentient beings" are words of the nine-part teachings; they are words of the incomplete teaching. Anger and joy, sickness and medicine, are all oneself; there is no one else. Where is there a Buddha appearing in the world? Where are there sentient beings to be saved? As the *Diamond Cutter Scripture* says, "In reality, there are no sentient beings who attain extinction and deliverance."

Not to love Buddhas or bodhisattvas, not to be affected by greed for anything existent or nonexistent, is called "saving others." Also not to keep dwelling in the self is called "saving oneself." Because the sicknesses are not the same, the medicines are not the same, and the prescriptions are also not the same—you should not one-sidedly hold fast (to any of them). If you depend on such things as Buddhas or bodhisattvas, all this is dependence upon the prescription. Therefore it is said, "One who has arrived at wisdom cannot be one-sided." That which is discussed in the teachings is likened to yellow leaves;[123] it is also like an empty fist deceiving a small child (pretending there is something in it). If someone does not realize this principle, this is called the same as ignorance. As it is said, "Bodhisattvas who practice transcendent wisdom should not grasp my words or depend on the commands of the teachings."

Anger is like a rock, love is like river water. Right now, just have no anger, no love; this is passing through mountains, rivers, and stone walls. Just to cure the illnesses of deaf worldlings, much learning and intellectual explanation cure the diseases of the eyes.

Going from humanity to Buddhahood is "gain," going from humanity to hell is "loss." "Right" and "wrong" are also the same. The third patriarch said, "Throw away gain and loss, right and wrong, all at once." When you don't keep clinging to anything existent or nonexistent, this is called not abiding in conditioning. When you do not even abide in nonabiding, this is called tolerance of not abiding in emptiness. To cling to oneself as Buddha, oneself as Ch'an or the Way, and make that an understanding, is called clinging to the inward view; attainment by causes and conditions, practice and realization, is called the outward view. Master Pao-chih said, "The inward view and the outward view are both mistaken."

When eye, ear, nose and tongue are each unaffected by greed for all things, existent or nonexistent, this is called "accepting and upholding a four line stanza."[124] It's also called the four attainments.[125] The six sense media without traces are also called the six superknowledges. Right now just do not be obstructed by any existent or nonexistent things; also do not abide in nonobstruction, and have no knowledge or understanding of nonabiding—this is called supernatural power. When you do not hold to this supernatural power, because it is called having no supernatural powers, it is like the saying, "The traces of the feet of a bodhisattva with no supernatural power cannot be found." This is someone beyond Buddha, the most inconceivable.

Humanity is oneself, divinity is wisdom's illumination. Praise is joy, rejoicing is in the objective realm. The realm is heaven, the praiser is humanity; humanity and heaven embrace each other, both can see each other.

Pure knowledge is heaven, correct knowledge is human. What is originally not Buddha, to others he said, "This is Buddha." This is called the knot of substance. Right now just do not create knowledge or understanding of Buddha, and also have no knowledge or understanding of nonabiding, this is called annihilation of the knot. It is also called true thusness, and it is called substantial thusness. If you seek Buddha, seek enlightenment, this is called manifesting body and mind. But right now as long as you have any thought of seeking at all, it's called manifesting body and mind. As it is said, "Although the quest for enlightenment is an excellent quest, it adds double to mundane troubles." Seeking Buddha is the mass of Buddhas; seeking all various things existent or nonexistent is the mass of sentient beings. But if the present mirror awareness just does not dwell on anything existent or nonexistent, this is "not entering into the categories of the masses."

Right now, in the midst of each sound, fragrance, flavor, feeling, phenomenon, and so forth, not to love and not to covet anything in any realm, just having none of the ten forms of defiled mind,[126] this is attaining Buddhahood on the basis of comprehension; studying the written word and seeking understanding is called the attainment of Buddhahood on the basis of conditions.[127] To see Buddha and know Buddha is possible, but if you say that Buddha knows, Buddha sees, Buddha hears, Buddha speaks, that's all right—seeing fire is possible, but it is impossible for fire to see; it's like a sword, which can cut things, but things cannot cut the sword.

People who know Buddha, people who see Buddha, people who speak of Buddha, are as numerous as the sands of the Ganges river; but as for those who are Buddha knowing, who are Buddha seeing, who are Buddha speaking, there is not one in ten thousand. Because one has no eyes himself he depends on another for eyes; in the teachings this is called deductive knowledge. Now if you covet knowledge and understanding of Buddha, this too is called deductive, inferential knowledge (not direct knowledge).

Wordly metaphor is by positive example; the incomplete teaching is by positive example. The complete teaching is by negative example; to "abandon your head, eyes, marrow and brain" is negative example. Now not craving such things as Buddhahood or enlightenment is negative example; that which is hard to abandon is likened to the head, eyes, marrow, and brain. If you shine fixedly upon all existent and nonexistent things, this is called the "head"; to be captured by any existent or nonexistent things is called "hands." The time before you have illumined the objects before you is called "marrow and brains."

In the sanctified state cultivating profane causes, a Buddha enters among sentient beings, becoming like them in kind to invite, lead, teach and guide them; joining those hungry spirits, his limbs and joints afire, he expounds the transcendence of wisdom to them, inspiring them with the will for enlightenment. If he only stayed in the sanctified state, how could he go there and talk with them? Buddha enters into various classes and makes a raft for sentient beings; like them he feels pain, unlimited toil and stress. When a Buddha enters a painful place, he too feels pain, the same as sentient beings; a Buddha is not the same as sentient beings only in that he is free to go or to stay. A Buddha is not empty space; feeling pain, how could he not suffer? If one says he does not suffer, these words are contradictory; do not speak idly and wrongly say that a Buddha's spiritual powers are free or not free. Other than praising a medicinal prescription, he does not want to have the ugliness of duality showing. The teachings say, "If a man places Buddha and enlightenment in the realm of affirmation, he incurs a great fault."

If in the presence of someone who doesn't know of Buddha, there is no fault in speaking this way. It is like undefiled cow's milk—that cow does not stay on the high plain, nor does it abide in the low marsh; this cow's milk can be medicine. The high plain symbolizes Buddhahood, the low marsh symbolizes sentient beings. As it is said, the real body of true wisdom of those who realize thusness no longer has this disease—their intellect and eloquence are uninhibited, free to leap up, unborn, imperishable; this is called birth, old age, sickness, and death.

Pain and suffering are darkness; having eaten mushroom soup, Shakyamuni Buddha suffered dysentery and met his end. This is darkness as repository; light reveals traces. With light and darkness all removed, do not grasp them. In nongrasping there is also no nongrasping. He is neither light nor dark—his birth in the royal palace, marriage to Yasodhara, and eight aspects of attainment to the Way,[128] are the judgments of the false conceptions of disciples and outsiders. Since it is said that his is not a body (nourished by) mixed food, Chunda[129] said, "I know the Realized One will certainly not accept or eat it."

Most important, it is necessary to have two eyes, to shine through the affairs of both sides. Do not just wear one eye and go on one side; for then there will be another side to arrive. The goddess of fortune and the girl of darkness accompany each other; a wise host does not admit either of them.

Right now, if your mind is like empty space, for the first time your study has some accomplishment. An eminent patriarch in India said, "The Himalaya is compared to great nirvana."[130] The first patriarch in this country, Bodhidharma, said, "Mind and mental conditions like wood or stone." The third patriarch said, "Immobile, forgetting conditions." Ts'ao-ch'i (the sixth patriarch) said, "Do not think good or bad at all." My late master (Ma-tsu) said, "Be like a lost man, unable to tell his whereabouts." Master Seng-chao said, "Shutting off knowledge, blocking perception, solitary awareness, something obscure and unfathomable."[131] Manjusri said, "Mind is like empty space, therefore respectful obeisance has nothing to look upon; the most profound scripture is neither heard nor accepted and upheld."

Right now if you just don't see or hear anything at all, existent or not, your six sense faculties shut off; if you can study in this way, if you can "uphold the scripture" in this way, then for the first time you have some accomplishment in practice. These words offend the ears and pain the mouth, but here if you can act this way until the second or third lifetime, then you can go to where there is no Buddha and manifest perfect enlightenment on the site of the Way, changing evil into good and good into evil, using evil ways to edify bodhisattvas of the tenth stage and using good ways to teach creatures of hell and hungry ghosts. Where there is illumination, you untie the bonds of illumination; in darkness you untie the bonds of darkness. Picking up gold and turning it into dirt, picking up dirt and turning it into gold, you can do a hundred things, transforming and playing freely.

Beyond worlds as numerous as river sands, if there is anyone who seeks deliverance, the Blessed One assumes the thirty-two marks of greatness and appears in front of them, speaking in the same language they do, expounding the truth for them, enlightening them according to their capacities, changing forms in response to beings, transforming and manifesting various dispositions, detached from "I" and "mine."

Yet these are all peripheral matters—this is still small function, and it is contained within the gate of Buddhist service. As for the great function, the great body hides in formlessness, the great sound is concealed in the rarified sound—like the fire within wood, like the sound of a bell or a drum, before the causes and conditions are fully present, you cannot speak of its existence or nonexistence. Whether born as an animal or in heaven, he abandons it like snot; bodhisattvas' ten thousand practices through six ways of transcendence are like riding a dead corpse to cross over to the shore, like being in a prison latrine hole and getting out. The Buddha puts on the thirty-two marks of a great being and calls them a robe of filth.

If you say that the Buddha absolutely does not experience the mortal cluster, you are in no way right. Buddha is not empty space—how could he absolutely not sense it? A Buddha is only different from sentient beings in that he is free to go or stay. Going from heavenly world to heavenly world, from Buddha field to Buddha field, is the constant practice of all enlightened ones.

It's like fire; seeing fire, just don't touch it with your hands, and the fire won't burn anyone. Right now just have none of the ten states of impure mind—greedy mind, lustful mind, defiled mind, angry mind, clinging mind, dwelling mind, dependent mind, attached mind, grasping mind, longing mind. But in each of these states there are the three stages, and then all your awareness and activity, whether they be transcendent or conventional, all movement and action, speech, silence, crying and laughing, all are enlightened wisdom. You have been standing a long time. Take care.

Question: What is the essential method for sudden enlightenment in the great vehicle?

The master said,

You all should first put an end to all involvements and lay to rest all concerns; do not remember or recollect anything at all, whether good or bad, mundane or transcendental—do not engage in thoughts. Let go of body and mind, set them free.

With mind like wood or stone, not explaining anything with the mouth, mind not going anywhere, then the mind ground becomes like space, wherein the sun of wisdom naturally appears. It is as though the clouds had opened and the sun emerged.

Just put an end to all fettering connections, and feelings of greed, hatred, craving, defilement and purity all come to an end. Unmoved in the face of the five desires and eight influences, not choked up by seeing, hearing, discerning or knowing, not confused by anything, naturally endowed with all virtues and the inconceivable use of all paranormal powers, this is someone who is free.

In the presence of all things in the environment, to have a mind neither still nor disturbed, neither concentrated nor distracted, passing through all sound and form without lingering or obstruction, is called being a wayfarer.

Not setting in motion good, evil, right or wrong, not clinging to a single thing, not rejecting a single thing, is called being a member of the great vehicle.

Not bound by any good or evil, emptiness or existence, defilement or purity, doing or nondoing, mundane or transcendental, virtue or knowledge, is called enlightened wisdom.

Once affirmation and negation, like and dislike, approval and disapproval, all various opinions and feelings come to an end and cannot bind you, then you are free wherever you may be; this is called a bodhisattva at the moment of inspiration immediately ascending to the stage of Buddhahood.

Question: How can one attain a mind which is like wood or stone in the presence of all situations?

The master said,

All various things have never of themselves spoken of emptiness; nor do they themselves speak of form, and they do not speak of right, wrong, defilement, or purity. Nor is there mind which binds and fetters people; it is just because people themselves give rise to vain and arbitrary attachments that they create so many kinds of understanding, produce so many kinds of opinion, and give rise to so many various loves and fears.

Just understand that the many things do not originate of themselves; all of them come into existence from one's own single mental impulse of imagination mistakenly clinging to appearances. If you know that mind and objects fundamentally do not contact each other, you will be set free on the spot. Each of the various things is in a state of quiescence right where it is; this very place is the site of enlightenment.

Inherent nature cannot be named; originally it is not mundane, nor is it holy; it is neither defiled nor pure. Also it is neither empty nor existent, and it is neither good nor bad. When it is involved with impure things, it is called the two vehicles of divinity and humanity. When the mind of purity and impurity is ended, it does not dwell in bondage, nor does it dwell in liberation; it has no mindfulness of doing, nondoing, bondage or liberation—then, though it is within birth and death, that mind is free; ultimately it does not comingle with all the vanities, the empty illusions, sensual passions, the mortal clusters and the elements of existence, life and death, or the sense media. Transcendent and without abode, nothing at all constrains it; it goes and comes through birth and death as through an open door.

When someone who is studying the Way comes in contact with various kinds of pain or pleasure, with things agreeable or disagreeable, his mind is not wearied; he does not think at all of fame, profit, clothing or food. He does not long for the benefits of merit and virtue; he is not hindered or obstructed by the various things of the world. Nothing is dear to him, nothing lovely; he is equanimous through pain and pleasure.

Simple clothing to keep off the cold, coarse food to sustain life; by unbending and intent, as though stupid, as though deaf and mute—then you will have some fulfillment. If in your mind you widely study knowledge and interpretation, seeking merit and seeking knowledge, all this is birth and death—it is of no benefit in respect to inner reality. On the contrary, blown up and down by the winds of understanding, you will return to the sea of birth and death.

A Buddha is one who does not seek; seek this and you turn away. The principle is the principle of nonseeking; seek it and you lose it. If you cling to nonseeking, this is still the same as seeking; if you cling to nondoing, this is the same again as doing. Therefore the *Diamond Cutter Scripture* says, "Do not grasp truth, do not grasp untruth, and do not grasp that which is not untrue." It also says, "The truth which those who realize thusness find has no reality or unreality."

If you are able to spend your whole life with a mind like wood or stone, then you will not be buoyed up and submerged by the mortal clusters, the elements of conscious existence, the media of sense, the five desires and eight winds. Then the cause of birth and death is cut off, and you are free to go or stay, unhindered by any causes or effects of doing; you will not be constrained by any indulgence. At that time to make a cause of causeless bondage, to share concerns as a benefactor,[132] to respond to all creatures with an unattached heart, to open all fetters with unhindered wisdom—this is called giving medicine according to the disease.

Question: Renunciants today, having received the precepts, are clean and pure in body and mouth; already invested with all the standards, do they attain liberation or not?
The master said, A little bit of liberation; but they have not yet attained liberation of mind and liberation in all places.

Question: What is liberation of mind and liberation in all places?
The master said,

Don't seek Buddha, don't seek the teaching, don't seek the community, and so forth; don't seek virtue and knowledge, intellectual understanding and so forth. When feelings of defilement and purity are ended, still don't hold to this non-seeking and consider it right—do not dwell at the point of ending, and do not long for heavens or fear hells. When you are unhindered by bondage or freedom, then this is called liberation of mind and body in all places.

You should not say you have a little bit of discipline, purity of body, mouth, and mind, and immediately consider that enough. You don't know that innumerable gates of discipline, concentration, wisdom, and nonindulgent liberation have never gotten involved with so much as a single hair.

Work hard! Henceforth you must take hold and investigate vigorously. Do not wait till your ears are deaf, your eyes dim, your face wrinkled and your hair white—when the pains of old age overtake your body, sadness and affection enshroud you, your eyes flow with tears, and in your heart is fear and dread. Without anything to rely upon at all, you do not know where you are going. At this time, you won't be able to coordinate your hands and feet; even if you have merit, knowledge, name, fame, profit and support, none of them will save you.

Because your mind's wisdom is not yet opened, you only think of various objects; you do not know how to reflect back, and you don't see the way of enlightenment. All the good and bad active affinities of your whole life will appear before you—you may be glad, you may be afraid; the mortal clusters of the six states of being will appear before you all at once, all spread with adornments, houses, boats, carts, brilliant shining light. Everything is what is manifest of the greed and craving of your own mind; all bad visions turn into surpassingly beautiful visions, but according to the heavy weight of greed and craving, compelled by your habitual active consciousness, you experience birth accompanied by attachments—you have no freedom at all. Whether you'll be a dragon or an animal, freeman or slave, is entirely uncertain.

Question: How is it possible to realize a share of freedom?
The master said,

Right now you have it if you have it. Otherwise, in the face of the five desires and eight winds, if there is no grasping or rejection in your feelings, when feelings of possessiveness, jealousy, greed and craving, of self and possessions, all come to an end, defilement and purity are both forgotten—you will be like the sun or moon in the sky, shining independently. When mind and mental conditions are like earth, wood, or stone, moment after moment, like saving your head were it ablaze, also like the great scent-bearing elephant crossing a river, cutting off the flow as he passes, causing there to be no doubt or error, this person neither heaven nor hell can contain.

APPENDIX A

*The three realms, or triple world,
containing various states of being
and planes of meditation and absorption*

REALM OF DESIRE:
>Hells; hungry ghosts; animals; titans; humans; six heavens of desires

REALM OF FORM:
>Unconscious heaven; heaven of brahma; heaven of fivefold pure abode (no troubles, no heat, good to see, good appearance, ultimate of form); four meditation heavens (joy and bliss, detachment from birth; joy and bliss, having settled nature; wondrous bliss, detachment from pain; pure and clear, giving up thought)

FORMLESS REALM:
>Four formless absorptions (infinity of space, infinity of consciousness, nothing at all, neither perception nor nonperception)

APPENDIX B

The eight consciousnesses and four wisdoms

1-5 sight, hearing, smell, taste, touch
6 cognitive consciousness
7 judgment and discrimination
8 storehouse consciousness, basic awareness

In the enlightened, these are "transmuted" into four wisdoms:
8th storehouse consciousness, becomes the "great round mirror wisdom"
7th *manas*, becomes the "wisdom of equality"
6th *manovijnana*, becomes the "wisdom of subtle analysis"
1–5 the basic sense consciousnesses, become the "wisdom of accomplishment"

BIBLIOGRAPHY

Texts on which the translation is based:

Hung-chou Pai-chang shan Ta-chih Ch'an-shih yu-lu (Pai-chang yu-lu)
Pai-chang kuang-lu

Nearly identical versions of these are found in the following Ch'an-Zen collections:
Ku-tsun-su yu-lu, "Collections of Sayings of Venerable Adepts of Old," a Sung dynasty anthology of collections of sayings and poetry of several dozen Ch'an masters from the eighth to the twelfth centuries.
Shike goroku, "Collections of Sayings of Four Masters," the extensive records of Ma-tsu, Pai-chang, Huang-po, and Lin-chi, four great figures of classical Ch'an. This collection was made in Japan in the seventeenth century, extracted

from a late Ming dynasty edition of the voluminous *Ku-tsun-su yu-lu*.

Zenshu sosho and *Zengaku taisei*, both collections containing the same materials, being Ch'an and Zen classics, mostly from China, presenting the original text in Chinese (the works originating in Japan are also written in Chinese) along with a transposition of the characters into Japanese order and inflection, with annotations.

Works consulted in the introduction:

Ching-te chuan-teng Lu, "Record of the Transmission of the Lamp," compiled during the Ching-te era of the Sung dynasty, around the year 1000, a sourcebook of Ch'an illustrative history from which many contemplation themes are drawn.

Kao-seng chuan er chi, "Biographies of Eminent Monks, second collection," by the great preceptual master and Buddhist historian Tao-hsuan, the seventh-century founder of the Nan-shan school of Vinaya in China. This is one of the most highly regarded works of Buddhist history of that period (4th–7th centuries) in China. It contains the earliest notice of the Ch'an patriarch Bodhidharma that is accepted by conventional historians, and observes that Bodhidharma was one of the only two meditation masters among all the meditation teachers of the day whose work survived in living transmission chains.

Leng-chia shih tzu chi, "Record of Teachers and Students of the Lankavatara," written by Ching-chao in the eight century, this is one of the earliest works on the early patriarchy of Ch'an. Written by a monk of the so-called Northern branch of Ch'an, it contains materials which seem to have been virtually unknown and not transmitted after the ninth century, when the Northern branch became quiescent.

Li-tai fa-pao chi, "Record of the Treasure of the Teaching in Successive Generations," another early account of the Ch'an patriarchy, also apparently from the eighth or ninth century, written by a monk of a stream of the Southern branch of Ch'an which worked in the remote regions of southwest China and also eventually became quiescent. Like other early accounts, this too contains materials not found in the traditions which later became common to the "southern" Ch'an which was transmitted by Ma-tsu and Shih-tou and eventually became the principal source of Ch'an teaching.

Lin-chien lu, "Annals of the Forest," a collection by the Sung dynasty Ch'an teacher Chiao-fan Te-hung, presenting a wide variety of materials with comments and observations by the author, who was also a man of learning, a noted author and poet, and a forthright critic. This collection includes live material from oral tradition and expresses views at variance with those customarily accepted or at least customarily unchallenged at that time.

Sung kao-seng chuan, "Sung Biographies of Eminent Monks," compiled in 988 by the monk Tsan-ning and others, this picks up the Ch'an patriarchy with the fifth patriarch Hung-jen, reckons Hui-neng as the sixth, and considers Pai-chang the de facto founder of Ch'an as a 'school' of Buddhism. As in the case of the earlier collection by Tao-hsuan, this *Biographies of Eminent Monks* covers the whole range of Buddhist activities under a number of rubrics, and only a fraction of the notices are of meditation and Ch'an masters; as these books were written as sort of reports to the emperor about the state of the Buddhist Sangha and the development of the religion, they naturally do not contain the esoteric lore of Ch'an, which sometimes appears to contain various kinds of history. Nevertheless, these *Biographies* contain informative and extraordinary material which sheds light on matters obscure in Ch'an recitals before the eleventh century.

RECORD OF SAYINGS OF PAI-CHANG

Footnotes

1. *Sila*, discipline or morality, *samadhi*, meditation, concentration, and *prajna*, wisdom or pure knowledge, are related to study of the *vinaya*, *sutra*, and *shastra* parts of the Buddhist canon, respectively, but these three studies are to be found in all types of Buddhist literature.

2. Ta-chi, "Great Quiescence," was a posthumous title given to Ma-tsu Tao-i (709–788). According to the *Sung Biographies of Eminent Monks*, Ancestor Ma (after his lay surname) was teaching in Nan-k'ang when Pai-chang came to him.

3. Hsi-t'ang Chih-tsang, "Treasury of Knowledge," (729–809) came to study with Ma-tsu when the great master was first teaching at Buddha's Footprint Range in Chi-an yang in Fukien province in the mid 740's. He stayed with Ma-tsu until the latter was invited to teach in the state-owned K'ai-yuan temple in the prefectural city dis-

trict of Hung-chou, around 777. One of Ma-tsu's senior disciples, he did not begin to teach until 791; eventually he had four enlightened successors.

4. Nan-ch'uan P'u-yuan, "Universal Prayer," (747–834), one of Ma-tsu's latest and greatest disciples, had studied the Buddhist teachings and practiced meditation for twenty years before he came to Ma-tsu and was "set free." With Ma-tsu in his last years Nan-ch'uan stood at the head of eight hundred disciples, and it is said that no one dared to question him. Around 795 he went up into Nan-ch'uan mountain in Chih-yang in Anhui province, where he scratched out his own livelihood from the mountainside, and practiced Ch'an for over thirty years without ever coming down from the mountain. Finally he accepted an invitation to "appear in the world" to teach, and always had several hundred students. He produced seventeen enlightened disciples, including the great Chao-chou Ts'ung-shen, (778–897), one of the most renowned of all ancient Ch'an masters.

5. Those who have entered the room are qualified successors, who have personally entered the "inmost sanctuary" of Ch'an, who have seen through everything and have witnessed reality with an enlightened guide. In Ch'an monasteries "entering the room" also refers to going to the teaching master for instruction or testing, and in general bears reference to the inner processes of the teacher-disciple relationship and the oral transmission of directions before and after enlightenment. Ma-tsu is said to have had well over a hundred enlightened disciples in all.

6. The version recorded in the *Ku-tsun-su yu-lu* up to this point is slightly different; see appendix to this translation.

7. "In what incident did you not accord (with reality, or the enlightened teacher)?" The Chinese word *yin-yuan*, "cause and condition," is used to mean "circumstances, event, incident," hence "story." Any *kung-an*, "public record" of Ch'an teachings in sayings and doings, are re-

ferred to as *yin-yuan*. The word for "accord" means "merging," "meshing," as of meeting minds, in this case; it is commonly used in Ch'an texts for understanding, realization.

8. A mat was placed in front of the teacher's seat in the teaching hall when he was teaching, where anyone who came forth from the crowd to ask a question would prostrate himself before and after. There are numerous forms of prostration and bowing; sometimes the word *bow* has been used for convenience to cover all. The rolling up of the mat signifies that the teacher's lecture is over and done.

9. *The Record of Sayings* also records an alternate version: "Ma-tsu said, 'Where are you coming and going?' The master said, 'Yesterday there happened to be an exit and entry; it is not worth pursuing.' Ma-tsu shouted once, whereupon the master left."

10. This famous incident is known as Pai-chang's second call on Ma-tsu; the previous *kung-an* about Pai-chang and the ducks is included as one of the main cases of the great Sung dynasty classic collection *Pi-yen-lu*, [Blue cliff record], and the second calling is told in the commentary on that story. The story of the second calling of Pai-chang on Ma-tsu is also told somewhat differently in the *Ku-tsun-su yu-lu*; see the appendix to this translation.

11. In no source is it clear whether there were one or several patrons or patron families. From the time of the Eastern Chin dynasty (4th century AD), with the great migrations of Chinese people to the south, the practice of "enclosure" by powerful families of natural resources such as mountains and swamps increased apace. After Ma-tsu's death, Pai-chang lived by Ma-tsu's grave for a time before he was invited to Hsin-wu. The patrons who offered the use of the mountain to the master seem to have left the community to itself there since there is no record of the doings of the patrons. The monks on Mt. Pai-chang evidently carried on their own building and farming.

12.   A *chang*, a unit of linear measure, equals ten *chih*, or Chinese feet; the number "hundred" in Chinese is often used to indicate an indefinitely large number. For convenience, in English the mountain might be called "Thousand Foot Mountain"; the name Ta-hsiung was the "proper name" of the mountain, the other a nickname.

13.   Kuei-shan Ling-yu (771–854) came to Pai-chang around 794 and spent many years there as chief cook for the community. When he first went to Kuei-shan, a remote mountain in the wilds of Hunan, it was uninhabited, and for years he "had only monkeys for companions and chestnuts for food." Eventually, with the help of villagers and monks coming from Pai-chang, a monastery was built on Kuei-shan, eventually becoming a leading center of Ch'an teaching.

14.   Huang-po Hsi-yun (d.855), a most remarkable Ch'an master, is said to have been seven feet tall, and had a round lump (considered a sign of greatness) on his forehead and a natural understanding of Ch'an. It is not known when he was born, and his early life is rather obscure: he also stayed in the congregations of Nan-ch'uan P'u-yuan and Yen-kuan Chi-an (both successors of Ma-tsu); while at Yen-kuan he served as chief monk, and met the future Emperor Hsuan-tsung, who was then hiding there. Huang-po once slapped Hsuan-tsung repeatedly in response to the latter's questions; after Hsuan-tsung had assumed the imperial throne, he bestowed on Huang-po the title "Coarse-Acting Monk." Huang-po is probably most famous for his little book *Essentials of the Transmission of Mind*, a series of lectures given in compliance with a request from prime minister P'ei-hsiu, a noted lay Ch'an devotee, and for being the teacher of the famous Lin-chi I-hsuan (d.866), whose lineage came to be known as the Lin-chi school of Ch'an.

15.   This could be read simply, "One day he took leave . . ." We have taken our reading according to the understanding of Yuan-wu K'e-ch'in in his commentary

on the eleventh case of the *Pi-yen-lu,* [Blue cliff record] (q.v.). The point in that context is Huang-po's brilliance and natural understanding of Ch'an. It is not clear how long Huang-po did eventually stay with Pai-chang, and there is no special record of his enlightenment there or anywhere else.

16.   A Ch'an master's "duty" is to pass on the transmission, or witness of enlightenment, to a worthy successor, who must in turn pass it on to students of yet a later generation. Hence the successor must "equal" the teacher by way of his own realization of the source, yet he must eventually "surpass" his teacher in order to renew the teaching for the benefit of others. With continuous variation of time, circumstance, and potential, a succession of true teachers cannot adhere to a mold, but must continually be surpassing their ancestors in order to meet the special needs of their own times and communities to successfully communicate the living reality of the Way. One evidence of this is the renewal of Ch'an teaching as manifest in the production of new literature and new techniques over the centuries. To "diminish the teacher's virtue by half" means that if the successor cannot pass on the transmission himself, his own teacher has in a sense failed to produce a complete heir, and half his virtue (helping others) is lacking (even though he has realized his own deliverance from confusion). This could be read, ". . .has less than half the teacher's virtue," focusing on the student, who cannot produce an heir equal to himself as his own teacher had at least done, according to this old saying.

17.   Yang-shan Hin-chi (d. 890) was first awakened by Tan-yuan Chen-ying, a successor of the renowned National Teacher Hui-chung (see *Blue Cliff Record,* case 18), an heir of the great sixth patriarch of Ch'an, Hui-neng. Yang-shan is said to have received (and destroyed) a book of ninety-seven circular symbols handed down to Tan-yuan from Hui-chung. Later Yang-shan was known for his use of circular figures in his teaching. He once said, "I attained the essence at Tan-yuan's; I attained the function at Kuei-

shan's." Yang-shan was also known as "Little Shakyamuni," an epithet first given him by an Indian or Central Asian monk who met him and said, "I came to China looking for Manjusri, but instead I found a little Shakyamuni." Manjusri is the bodhisattva representing pure wisdom and knowledge, said to reside on Mt. Wu-tai in northern China; this mountain became a pilgrimage place not only for Chinese, but for Tibetans, Mongolians, and other Central Asian Buddhists. Shakyamuni, of course, was the historical Buddha Gautama. Yang-shan was Kuei-shan's foremost disciple, and their transmission lineage came to be called Kuei-yang.

18.   See *Blue Cliff Record*, case 26, for a detailed treatment of this story.

19.   The esoteric meaning of father and mother is ignorance and lust.

20.   Another version has it that he drove them out with his staff, then called them back. The texts do not make clear whether this is "once" or "sometimes." Ma-tsu used to do this kind of thing; one of his heirs, Wu-yeh, was suddenly enlightened when Ma-tsu called to him and said, "What is it?" and Wu-yeh turned to look.

21.   The scene of this action is unclear, there being certain ambiguities in the words. There is evidence of a custom in some places to excuse a monk from *p'u-ch'ing*, "general labor," on the day of his awakening. Here it could be that Pai-chang "turned to" Huang-po as they both were going into the fields, and at the end Huang-po "went off." Or Huang-po might have been back in the meditation hall or elsewhere enjoying his enlightenment. Several stories of Huang-po's heir Lin-chi tell of him sleeping instead of sitting, loafing at work, breaking the summer retreat; they are supposed to show the aspect of transcendence and unconcern.

22.   This story is retold up to this point in the famous *kung-an* collection *Wu-men-kuan* (Mumonkan) [Gateless

gate], where it immediately follows Chao-chou's "No." A wild fox, or wild fox spirit, came to be a term critical of those who indulge in cleverness or try to claim personal liberty by repudiating cause and effect in their actions. The antinomian interpretation of Ch'an/Zen, popular in some quarters, is an example of "wild-fox Zen." This term can also be used, however, as a term of praise for one who actually realizes freedom of thought and action. The "red-bearded barbarian" originally alludes to Bodhidharma, the Ch'an patriarch who came to China in the fifth century; he was also called the blue-eyed barbarian, again alluding to the fact that he was not Chinese. Here the expression symbolizes an enlightened man and refers finally to Huang-po; this is Pai-chang's approval of Huang-po, who caught a wild fox alive. The word "barbarian" in Chinese means "not of the Han race"; in Ch'an it is not intended as a slur, as it might have been in conventional Chinese usage— rather, (besides referring to the non-Chinese ancestral teachers) it refers to the "true man of no status," one beyond the usual conventions.

23.   An itinerant ascetic named Ssu-ma, versed in geomancy, physiognomy, and meditation, is said to have suggested to Pai-chang to send Kuei-shan (the monk Ling-you) to live on Kuei-shan (Mt. Kuei in Hunan). According to the Ch'an history *Ching-te chuan-teng lu*, this Ssu-ma's advice was often taken in founding monasteries.

24.   The sound seer is Avalokitesvara, bodhisattva of universal compassion, known in Chinese as the observer of the sounds of the world. According to the *Surangama* scripture, he entered truth by audition, forgetting knowing and turning to the source. According to the *Chih-yueh lu*, this monk was Kuei-shan.

25.   Chang-ching Huai-yun (?–818) was another enlightened successor of the great teacher Ma-tsu. The place where he taught was near Ch'ang-an, the western capital of China in T'ang times, in northwestern China very far on foot from Pai-chang in the mountains of Kiangsi. Ch'an students were sometimes sent on such journeys for their

development, often carrying a certain saying, message, or instruction in their minds during the journey to see another enlightened master. Chang-ching was an accomplished teacher who had sixteen enlightened disciples in his lifetime.

26. Wu-feng Ch'ang-Kuan (nd.) was one of Pai-chang's successors. Hardly anything is known of him. Yun-yen T'an-sheng (781–841) stayed with Pai-chang for twenty years and later became enlightened in the presence of Yao-shan Wei-yen, an heir of Ma-tsu's contemporary Shih-t'ou. Yun-yen was Pai-chang's attendant for a long time, and it is said he never lay down for forty years; he later was the teacher of the famous Tung-shan Liang-chieh (807–869), who found Yun-yen with the help of Kuei-shan. Yun-yen thus was the ancestor of so-called Ts'ao-tung/Soto ways of Ch'an/Zen.

The series of questions and answers here is an instance of guidance "in the room" and is discussed in some detail in cases 70, 71, and 72 of the *Pi-yen-lu* (see the *Blue Cliff Record*, volume 3.)

EXTENSIVE RECORD OF PAI-CHANG

Footnotes

1. Literally "black and white"; this also has such meanings as ordained and lay, initiate and naive, profound and obvious.

2. From the standpoint of Mahayana, or great-vehicle Buddhism, all the scriptures of the lesser vehicle belong to the incomplete teaching, which is supposed to prepare people for the complete teaching. Within the great vehicle, there are various classifications of scriptures and doctrines in these terms, differing somewhat according to school. Pai-chang's interpretation does not seem to follow any of the doctrinal Buddhist schools strictly, and even includes all formal doctrine ultimately within the scope of the incomplete teaching.

3. The first book of the *Saddharmapundarika sutra* (hereafter referred to as the *Lotus Scripture*), on useful techniques to aid enlightenment, says, "I expain this nine-part

teaching according to the potentials of sentient beings; it is basically so they may enter the great vehicle that I explain this (Lotus) scripture." In the *Mahaparinirvana sutra* [Scripture of the great decease], part V, it says, "The 'half word' is called the nine-part teaching." "Nine-part" means nine of the twelve parts of the Buddhist canon, and has the sense of the lesser vehicle, or initiatory or incomplete teaching, the manifest aspect of the primitive Buddhist teachings. There are various classifications, but the classical enumerations of the nine-part teaching are that of the *Lotus Scripture*, which gives the southern tradition, or nine-part teaching of the lesser vehicle, and that of the *Scripture of the Great Decease*, which gives the classification of the northern tradition, or nine-part teaching of the greater vehicle, which is still not complete (lesser-vehicle Buddhism was not really repudiated but included by the great vehicle; the seeds of all phases of Buddhist teachings are actually found in all other phases). The incomplete teaching is so called because it has different meanings in different times, places, and human situations; its meaning is not definitive even when it is expressed as such because of its specific context. The complete teaching actually encompasses the aspect result of the proper application and interpretation of the incomplete teaching, and is as true as true can be. In T'ien-t'ai and Ch'an Buddhism, teachings are also called temporary/provisional and/or real and true; in Ch'an the constant light of transcendent wisdom and certain knowledge is called illumination or shining, while specific acts of expression in a given teaching situation are called function. All these distinctions have to do with practical application of an existing body of teaching material, "living and dead."

4. To leave home means to renounce the conventional ties of family and society; traditionally this refers generally to mendicancy and the homeless life or monkhood, but really means nonattachment to anything in the world. Lin-chi, the famous spiritual grandson of Pai-chang, said that even if one leaves civilian society to become ordained and just pursues attainments of some kind

without having a true and veritable knowledge and insight into reality, one is merely leaving one house to enter another.

5.   Vimalakirti and the great hero Fu were two famous laymen. Vimalakirti is considered to have been a fully-enlightened Buddha; a well-known scripture contains some of his teachings. He is said to have been a contemporary of Shakyamuni Buddha, but is regarded as transhistorical by many people. Fu, on the other hand, also called Shan-hui, was called a *mahasattva*, or great spiritual insight, and was widely considered an appearance of the future Buddha Maitreya, the Loving One, during and after his lifetime in eastern China in the years 497 to 570.

Vimalakirti means "pure name," and may be said to represent a Buddha in the world unstained by the world. In the *Vimalakirtinirdesa sutra*, [Discourse of Vimalakirti], a popular Mahayana Buddhist book, he chides saints and bodhisattvas for clinging to the teaching and their practices, for indulging in a sense of righteousness or holiness; in this respect Pai-chang resembles Vimalakirti.

Mahasattva Fu was a small farmer with a wife and two children when he began to study Buddhism seriously and meditate at the age of twenty-four, while still supporting himself and family by working days on a mountainside field. He used to meditate and eventually teach during the nights, working by day; he had many extraordinary visions and experiences, and many people believed in him. After a certain vision, Fu gave up all he had to provide for a 'non-prohibitive feast', a communal feast instituted by Buddhists in which any sentient being was allowed to share. In a Buddhist kingdom such as southeast China was then, this institution was a good way to redistribute taxes to the poor and needy; Mahasattva Fu tried to persuade Emperor Wu of the Liang dynasty to establish communal feasts on a regular basis, six times a month, but apparently without success. Fu continued to work at farming with his family and some disciples; excess food left over from his fasts he gave to the hungry, and continued to donate money and goods from his fields to the poor. Three times he sold

Sayings and Doings of Pai-chang

everything he had, whether given to him or earned by his labor, to set up great nonprohibitive feasts. He even sold his wife and children and hired himself out as a worker, but such was his repute that evidently his family and some land were "bought" by well wishers who never took possession. This Fu was indeed a man in the world who was beyond measure; that he was considered a spiritual hero and future Buddha in those oppressive and perilous times is reasonable.

6. The derivation of this word connotes work, effort, striving to quiet the passions, purification of will, poverty and mendicancy.

7. Three replies, acknowledgements, agreements, to each of a number of statements is a democratic form used in ancient Buddhist communities for obtaining the consent of the community on important issues, and in important observances such as open confession and repentance, and ordination, transmission of the Buddhist precepts. A novice will be asked if he accepts each precept one by one (or, later, one or everyone will be asked if they are faultless in observing each precept), to which one must reply three times giving assent. To ask for or consent to anything three times indicates a firm commitment. In outward form, the complete discipline is the traditional vinaya, which explains about 250 precepts for monks and 348 for nuns, but it also means that the heart is really tamed and discipline empowers everything one does. A number of famous Ch'an masters were never ordained, or were not fully ordained until after their enlightenment.

8. The derivation of this term can include many kinds of speech that are deemed improper according to Buddhist behavioral ethics; according to the well-known *Abhidharmakosha*, all words which come forth from a defiled or attached mind are so considered—it can be flattery, deceit, etc. In this case, once the teaching of the way of enlightenment is being practiced, to speak in terms of something being attained is 'suggestive talk.'

9. By this Pai-chang means all things within the realms of thought, imagination, experience, anything that can be referred to even hypothetically by any logical proposition such as 'it exists' or 'it does not exist' or 'it may or may not exist.'

10. The two vehicles here are that of disciples (*sravaka*, "hearers [of the Buddha's voice]") and that of self-enlightened sages (*pratyekabuddha*). There are traditionally said to be four fruits of discipleship—stream enterer, once returner (who returns to the mundane life once), non-returner, and saint (who has realized nirvana). Self-enlightened sages realize personal liberty by applied comprehension of the chain of cause and effect of becoming, from ignorance to old age and death, rooting out passions and abiding in extinction. Pai-chang uses the terms in the sense of those who have really arrived in these states. These two vehicles are considered both part of the so-called lesser vehicle because they only realize the emptiness of persons without realizing the emptiness of things, remain in the "deep pit of liberation," able only to leave the world of passion, unable to effectively return to it out of compassion to help others realize liberation.

11. Or "immaterial realm," where there are no images, no sense of matter. In the traditional Buddhist conception of three realms (or triple world) of desire, form, and formlessness, the last is considered most sublime, realm of the highest meditative attainments. From ancient times it has been said that people who reached this realm often thought they had attained real nirvana and grasped nothingness as their view, giving rise to the idea that they were better than they really were, that there was nothing beyond what they had realized. In the *Lotus Scripture*, which introduces the idea of one sole vehicle of which the two and three vehicles are partial revelations for elementary and middling capacities, nirvana is called an illusory citadel which the Buddhas showed to those of the two vehicles as a temporary resting place, so that in their weakness they would not be frightened or wearied by the

prospect of the infinite path of perception and knowledge of enlightenment which is their destiny.

12.   Shedding a Buddha's blood is one of the five or seven deadly crimes, which incur instant and unremitting consequences. Pai-chang here uses the term in its esoteric sense of remaining attached to subjective emptiness and nothingness, thus failing to unfold the full potential of innate, active Buddhahood, thus "obstructing the Buddha's light" and killing the Buddha.

13.   Or, "good in the beginning." Shakyamuni Buddha said the Dharma is good in the beginning, good in the middle, good in the end. We translate according to Pai-chang's use of these terms in describing personal and mass development of the process and history of the Way of the Buddhas, the enlightened ones.

14.   The Dharma, the teaching, is likened to a raft which carries beings over the ocean of suffering of birth and death to the peaceful "other shore" of nirvana. The followers of the great vehicle criticized those of the so-called lesser vehicle for clinging to the letter of the Dharma, even for clinging to understanding, like one who reaches the other shore but will not leave the raft behind and drags it with him. Such are they who cling to cultivated practice and acquired understanding—they are called disciples because they still hold to something, still follow something.

15.   The half-word teaching refers to this nine-part teaching, or incomplete teachings of the great vehicle. See above.

16.   *Mara* (translated as "demon" or "delusion") is "the killer," meaning any sort of passion, attachment, or hindrance, or the object or cause thereof. There are many enumerations of *mara* in scriptures and treatises, but in a broad sense anything can be a demon or delusion. Some well-known *mara* are afflictions, components of the mortal being, death, and Papiyan, the Evil One, who is called the king of demons and whose palace is in the sixth heaven of

desire where he freely enjoys the delights produced in other sense heavens. The king of demons or delusion esoterically alludes to the sixth sense, the conceptual consciousness, which organizes the data of the five elementary senses.

17. Apart from hallucinations and other shallow states usually considered abnormal but common in meditation, especially in the beginning, meditation sickness also involves profound attachment and blindness or partiality induced by absorption in meditation states. Regarding the point Pai-chang is making here, consider the words of Takusui, a Japanese Zen meditation master:

> The disease of submergence is most difficult to know. Of those who work on meditation, eight or nine out of ten retain the disease of submergence and bring about calamity. This is not sleep, and there is no distraction; it seems as if all thoughts of errant imagination were ended, and one is joyful, happy, pure and clear; one may sit for a long time without weariness, heaven and earth seem equal, one thinks it is neither void nor silent, neither existent nor nonexistent, neither right nor wrong. There are those who retain this and think it is awakening to the Way. It is greatly to be feared; when you remain here, henceforth you will fall into a false path. (*Zokuzenmonhogoshu*, *Takusui kanahogo*, 53–54)

18. That is, being bounded by what is known (and by one's station or practice). Without basic equanimity, discriminating knowledge is a fetter; one term for sudden awakening is "forgetting one's knowledge." Yun-men said, "Why do we speak of the special transmission outside of the teachings? If you attain by learned interpretation and intellectual knowledge, you're like the sages of the tenth state of bodhisattvahood who expound Dharma

like clouds and rain, yet are still scolded because their seeing of reality is as though screened by gauze." (*Ching-te Chuan-teng lu* 19)

19. Or, ignorance (because of) objective knowledge (what is known); ignorance (which is knowledge). In the *Scripture on the Stage of Enlightenment (Fo-ti-ching)*, this is phrased to suggest ignorance of subtle and extremely subtle knowledge, meaning that the knowledge of Buddhas is beyond conventional knowledge, however sophisticated. The Ch'an explanation of this actually has the same meaning, though it is phrased in reverse, emphasizing the inconceivability not only of "the other side," absolute nirvana, but of "this side," absolute nirvana in life and death. Nan-ch'uan says, "According to the explanation, warriors for enlightenment dwell in the meditation of the heroic march *(surangamasamadhi)* and find the secret treasury of the teachings of all the enlightened ones, naturally attaining all stations of meditation, liberation, and the inconceivable function of supernormal powers. They go to all worlds, everywhere manifesting a material body to show the true awakening of an enlightened being, turn the great wheel of the true teaching and enter nirvana, cause the illimitable to enter a pore, propound a one-phrase scripture for countless eons without ever exhausting its meanings, teach innumerable hundreds of millions of sentient beings, and realize acceptance of the nonorigination of all things. This is still called the 'folly of knowledge,' 'the folly of extremely refined knowledge'—it is completely contrary to the Way" (*Ku-tsun-su yu-lu* 12). Nan-ch'uan also used to say, "Where knowledge cannot reach, do not try to speak of." It is often said that Buddhas do not consciously know they are Buddhas except when they share the world of sentient beings, for there is no enlightenment without delusion. Also, intellectual knowledge can also be a barrier and a folly if it convinces people they have realized something when in reality they haven't put it into practice.

20. The derivation of the word rendered as both "phases" and "states" is the same, a case where Sanskrit

influenced Chinese use of words. Sanskrit *pada* can mean "phase" and is so translated by Chinese *ju*, but can also mean, among other things, "a station or position." Pai-chang uses the *ju* to refer to formulae or expressions of teachings, which also represent states of realization or phases of development. All propositions of logic, such as existence or nonexistence, are *ju*, statements or propositions, but are also used to refer to existence or nonexistence themselves or of things, given the conventional supposition that there are subjective and objective realities with definite correspondence.

21. Dipankara, whose name means "burning lamp," was an ancient Buddha in whose presence Shakyamuni is said to have originally been inspired to realize enlightenment. The burning lamp can represent the basic energy of awareness illuminating all; a Buddha succeeding to this burning lamp is a historical Buddha, a Buddha in the world.

22. *Wind* means influence, way, appearance, style; here it means the charisma or influence, the acts or ability of an enlightened personality.

23. Virtue and knowledge are said to be the two provisions for the way to enlightenment; virtue, or merit, is said to help the development of knowledge, or wisdom. Five among the well-known six *paramita* or ways of transcendence—generosity, morality, forbearance, effort, and meditation—are said to be part of the store of virtue; the sixth, wisdom, is of the store of knowledge.

24. In the *Scripture Spoken by Vimalakirti*, Purnamaitrayaniputra, most eloquent of Shakyamuni Buddha's disciples, relates that once as he was teaching new mendicants, Vimalakirti said to him 'Hey Purna! You should first enter meditative concentration to observe the minds of these people, and only then explain the Way to them. You shouldn't put impure food in a precious vessel. You should know such is the state of awareness of these mendicants' minds, and compare lapis lazuli to quartz. You are ignor-

ant of the basic source of sentient beings; you cannot inspire these people with the way of the lesser vehicle—*They themselves have no wounds, so don't wound them.* If you want to travel the great Way, do not point out a little path. No one can put the ocean in an ox track, and none can compare the light of the sun to that of a firefly.' (book 3 of Kumarajiva's translation) The lapis lazuli, great Way, ocean and sunlight refer to the great vehicle of universal Buddhahood, whereas the crystal, ox-track puddle, and firefly light refer to the lesser vehicle, which concentrates on extinction of egoism, passion and affliction, and on realization of sainthood and release from mundane concerns. Here Pai-chang is talking about liberation, so that all concepts of theory, practice, and attainment all fall into perspective as part of the incomplete, or inductive teaching, and are dropped by the free, as the "dust of Dharma." Then they can see directly and act accordingly without remaining within fixed standards. Mahayana Buddhists say that those of the lesser vehicle do not fully realize the universal enlightened nature; in Ch'an it is said that pursuit of a formal state of Buddhahood or whatever will hinder one from realizing innate enlightenment.

25.   The tenth and highest stage of bodhisattvahood in the struggle for enlightenment is, according to the *Avatamsaka sutra*, a state in which one teaches for the benefit of sentient beings; it is called Dharmamegha, "clouds of Dharma," their teaching profuse as rain, falling upon and enriching the bodhisattvas in the lesser stages and the beings in other estates.

26.   Shariputra was foremost in wisdom, Mahamaudgalyayana was foremost in supernormal powers, Mahakasyapa foremost in asceticism (he is traditionally considered the first Indian patriarch of Ch'an, after Shakyamuni), Subhuti foremost in realization of emptiness and noncontention, Purnamaitrayaniputra foremost in eloquence in explanation, Mahakatyayana foremost in argument, Aniruddha foremost in clairvoyance, Upali foremost in moral discipline (he recited the vinaya at the

first Buddhist council after Shakyamuni's death), Rahula (natural son of Shakyamuni) foremost in meticulous practice, and Ananda, foremost in learning (he recited the sutras at the first council and is considered the second patriarch of Ch'an and all schools of Buddhism). Sunakshatra, also said to be a blood son of the Buddha Shakyamuni, learned the teachings and attained the fourth state of meditation (see below) but thought that was nirvana, became conceited, and eventually regressed and joined the outsiders. Lin-chi said, "Sunakshatra knew the whole canon yet fell living into hell; the earth couldn't hold him in his conceit."

27.   The four stages of meditation (Sanskrit: *dhyana*; Chinese: *channa*) are in the realm of form, purely aesthetic without values attached to forms, no emotional interpretations; the meditations cut off the confusion of the realm of desire. With the first meditation comes emptiness, light, stability, knowledge, good will, gentleness, joy, bliss, and conformity with the environment; it is supported by five branches, of contemplation, judgment, joy, bliss, and single-mindedness. The second stage abandons the contemplation and judgment of the first; it has four branches, inner purity, joy, bliss, and single-mindedness. The third stage abandons the sense of joy; it comprises indifference, recollection, discernment, bliss, and single-mindedness. The fourth excludes the sense of bliss; its four branches are neither pain nor bliss, relinquishment, single-mindedness. These are futher described in terms of eighteen heavens. The four stages of meditation are said to have leakage (that is, some kind of impulse, passion, attachment, however subtle) and do not lead to true nirvana, only to heavenly states. The eight absorptions (also called concentrations, attainments, samadhi, *samapatti*) are the four meditational stages in the realm of form plus four formless absorptions—absorption in infinity of space, infinity of consciousness, in absence of anything at all, and in neither perception nor nonperception. Beyond this there is the total cutting off of all sense and perception, but none of

these are nirvana; they are not permanent, and in Buddhism are not considered goals—as in some Yogic traditions—but rather tools. The states of formless absorption are said to last for twenty to eighty thousand eons.

28. This saying is from the *Mahavaipulyamahasamnipata sutra* (Chinese: *Ta-chi ching*) [Great collection scripture], book 18, and is rather common in Ch'an sayings. It does not mean that there is no liberation for bodhisattvas, only that they regard the enlightenment of all beings as the only really complete enlightenment, and do not succumb to the peace of decease while they can still actively help awaken and liberate others. At a certain stage of the Way, which is still shallow but seems more profound than anything that has gone before, the wayfarer will tend to seek out quiet, especially if alone, and will suffer even more than before when encountering the ordinary turmoil and confusion, lust, rage, and folly of the world; thus it is said that finest ghee is like poison to a saint.

29. These are archetypical bodhisattvas, warriors for enlightenment, dedicated to the enlightenment of all beings. Manjusri represents wisdom and knowledge, Avalokitesvara represents compassion, and Mahasthamaprapta represents empowerment. Traditionally Manjusri is said to dwell on Mt. Wu-tai (also called Ch'ing-liang) in northern China; Avalokitesvara is said to have first appeared in China on P'u-t'o island of Ning-po. Manjusri is usually paired with Samantabhadra, who represents principle, meditation, and action. Avalokitesvara and Mahasthamaprapta are usually represented at the left and right sides of Amitabha, the Buddha of infinite light and life, guarding his compassion and knowledge. These and other bodhisattvas appear in legend and history in the Far East in various guises, from mysterious beggars to famous Buddhists (cf. *Blue Cliff Record*, case 35); a number of great masters of various schools were said to be manifestations of transhistorical bodhisattvas.

30. The *Samyukta agama* says, "Stream enterers are perfect in four ways; they do not defile the purity of the enlightened ones, the teachings, or the community, and are perfect in the precepts of the saints, and always accept and maintain this as is." (ch. 33) (*Taisho* 2, 339b).

31. Avalokitesvara, for example, is described as appearing in whatever form suitable to rescue beings from their troubles anywhere. The twenty-fifth book of the *Lotus Scripture* (in Kumarajiva translation) is called "The Universal Gate of the Bodhisattva Who Watches Over the Sounds of the World," and it says, "If there are beings of a land who could be delivered by means of a Buddha body, Avalokitesvara Bodhisattva then manifests the body of a Buddha to expound the Dharma for them. For those who could be delivered by the body of a self-enlightened sage, he manifests the body of a solitary Buddha to expound the Dharma for them. For those who could be delivered by a disciple, he manifests the body of a disciple to expound the Dharma." It goes on to enumerate various other states of being, including those represented by Hindu deities, in the same formula, using appropriate forms, appearances, languages, and customs, to deliver a universal message to myriad different situations, representing all-sided compassion, with "a thousand eyes on a thousand hands." Ultimately Avalokitesvara may be said to represent the unconditional, objectless compassion of the body of reality, ultimate emptiness and rest, but joining sentient beings in their tasks in order to help them is one of the traditional acts of solidarity practiced by bodhisattvas.

32. From Seng-chao's treatise, "Nirvana Has No Name." Seng-chao (384–414) was an outstanding disciple of the famous translator Kumarajiva (344–413). He had been a fan of the ancient Taoist classics as a literate but poor youth who earned a living copying books, but devoted himself to Buddhist studies when he read the old translation of the scripture spoken by Vimalakirti. With Kumarajiva he studied the works of Nagarjuna, fourteenth patriarch of Ch'an in India and the inspiring genius of the

Madyamaka or "middle way" of Buddhism in the early part of the first millenium C.E. The treatises of Seng-chao, Nagarjuna, and the transcendence of wisdom scriptures which inspired him were all widely appreciated in Ch'an circles.

33.   Literally, "demon talk" or "devil talk". This is not necessarily inside or outside; it can refer to teachers and teachings which have attachments, or one's own delusions or persuasions reflecting such influences.

34.   These are vows to rescue all sentient beings, cut off all afflictions, study the infinite approaches to truth, and fulfill the unexcelled way of enlightenment.

35.   Afflicted, affected, or defiled, is the sense of a term meaning "leak" in Chinese, referring to passion, attachment, mind-wandering and "leaking" out of right mindfulness to play upon external things or internal feelings. Good deeds done with a sense of accomplishment may be said to be afflicted. In later Ch'an idiom, "leaking and tarrying" can variously mean indulging, spilling your guts, or making an effort out of compassion.

36.   "Hundred volumes of *veda*"—the Chinese had scant knowledge of the classical Indian vedas, and Pai-chang seems to use this word in its semantic sense of "knowledge." "Hundred" stands for an indefinitely large number. Later Pai-chang speaks of twelve veda books or books of knowledge, evidently referring to the Buddhist canon, which has twelve parts.

37.   Expressions of greed, lust, defilement, anger, clinging, dwelling, dependence, attachment, grasping, and affection. These are the persuasions of demons.

38.   This common expression comes from the *Hsiao-ching*, [Classic of filial piety], and is proverbial for the wise and righteous.

39.   The mystic mirror of the cosmos of adornment reflects all the qualities of the cosmos, each of which reflects

each and every particular feature of the cosmos. This image was also used in the Hua-yen school, based on the *Avatamsaka sutra*, said to have been spoken from the ocean-reflection absorption, in which everything is reflected like stars in the ocean.

40. All who seek something, especially with a sense of acquisition, are called "outsiders" or "heretics." After his birth the Buddha Shakyamuni is said to have looked all around, pointed up and down and said, "In the heavens and on earth, I alone am the honored one." This is taken to refer to absolute unity of being, Shakyamuni being said to have realized the way simultaneously with all beings, and to the universal, innate, enlightened nature, beyond which there is nothing to seek. As Pai-chang says, his statement is just to eliminate dualism; it is not glorification of an individual or a religion.

41. They are relatively easy to understand, there being a guide, and they are primarily concerned with self-cultivation and individual salvation; hence these expressions of the Way are said to carry a relatively light burden.

42. *Dust* is also used to refer to fields ("objects" or "data") of sense; sometimes itself it carries the sense of defilement, being the stuff of mundane turmoil, but sometimes it is clearly neutral. The word for "teachings" also means things or the field of the sixth or conceptual sense. In the expression here, "defilement" is actually added to "dust" in the Chinese; sometimes Pai-chang also speaks of "affliction by the dust of Dharma," which could also mean any thing, principle, way, etc., defiled or pure, though Pai-chang is specific in his use.

43. Buddhas, enlightened ones, saints and those struggling for universal enlightenment are all called fields of merit, having accumulated virtue in all their ways. It is said that if one gives to them, merit or blessings grow from this liberality. Since Buddhas and bodhisattvas dedicate all their virtues to the welfare of sentient beings, they are fields of blessings for beings; Buddhahood has no fixed

limits since it comprehends the struggles of others and by cultivation of virtue and knowledge becomes a treasure for all beings.

44. Host and guest can refer to enlightenment and delusion, teacher and student, complete teaching and incomplete teachings, absolute and relative. It is necessary to discern the point of view and the audience to understand and appreciate the words of the teachings. Sometimes sayings have both host and guest applications, simultaneously present or visible in practical sequence. Lin-chi speaks of host facing host, host facing guest, guest facing host; these allude to states or perceptions and can also be used to describe specific *kung-an* or Ch'an stories.

45. This comes from the writings of Seng-chao.

46. Buddha, Dharma, and Sangha, the three treasures of Buddhism.

47. The vehicles of discipleship, self-enlightenment, and the heroic struggle for universal enlightenment (sravakayana, pratyekabuddhayana, bodhisattvayana) are provisionally distinguished within the unique vehicle of enlightened knowledge because of confusion among sentient beings, so all may benefit according to their capacity to understand and apply the teachings.

48. A relatively rare third person pronoun (*ch'u*) is often used in Ch'an literature to refer to reality, thusness. Tung-shan said, "I am not It—It is really me."

49. The five places are the five senses; when afflicted with greed, the mind itself is the king demon and his abode is in the realm of desire. Mention of the divination and elemental signs here does not allude to an occult science, but is merely a simile for bondage in a certain sphere or arrangement because of conceptual or sensual dogmatism.

50. This is from the *Vajracchedika prajnaparamita sutra*, [Diamond-cutter scripture], which emphasizes the trans-

cendence of wisdom, going beyond all sense of principle, practice, and attainment once they have been actualized; hence the metaphor of leaving behind the raft when the other shore is reached.

51.   Titans are waning gods, still powerful, but generally characterised by anger, resentment, contention. In a static cosmology the titans (*asura*) would correspond roughly to the Eddic frost giants, always waging battle against the celestial forces, trying to take over paradise. The story of the battle between Indra and the titans appears in the *Avatamsaka (Ch: Hua-yen) sutra*. Lin-chi, Pai-chang's spiritual grandson, uses the story to make a similar point: "You say Buddhas have six powers which are inconceivable. All the gods, the sublimated sorcerers, titans, and spirits of great power also have supernatural powers, but could they be Buddhas? Wayfarers, do not misunderstand. When the king of titans battled with Indra, he was defeated and led his 84,000 followers into the hole of a lotus root to hide. Was he not supernatural? What I have cited here are all powers from action, dependent powers. A Buddha's six powers are otherwise; he enters form without being confused by form, enters sound without being confused by sound, enters smell without being confused by smell, enters taste without being confused by taste, enters feeling without being confused by feeling, enters phenomena without being confused by phenomena." (*Lin-chi lu, Chih-chung* 10). Various powers and wonders experienced in meditation can in fact be hindrances to enlightenment if the practitioner, convinced of his attainment, is waylaid by the extraordinary.

52.   Fundamental illusion and arousal are two of three "subtle aspects" of ignorance. Fundamental illusion is also called action in ignorance, or simply action, and is defined as the initial stirring of the mind ignorant of the true nature of reality. The aspect of arousal is called the seer or perceiver, and results from the movement of the mind. The third subtle aspect is the seen or objective, and is correlative to the seer; with the appearance of this subtle aspect,

the division of subject and object appears.

Following the appearance of these three subtle aspects are six so-called coarse aspects of ignorance: knowing, continuing, grasping, naming, initiation of doings, entanglement, and suffering.

53. From most ancient times in Buddhism it has been said that all good and bad come from the mind; whether a matter of judgment or action, all proceeds from the state of mind, so a pure mind leads to pure deeds. In Ch'an and Zen teaching the ultimate precept or discipline is the mind without contrivance; this is called the formless discipline of the mind ground.

54. The thirty-two marks and eighty refinements of greatness here refer to the so-called beatified body of a Buddha, experiencing the fruits of discipline, meditation, and knowledge; the physical graces and excellences represented are said to be the result of selfless virtuous actions, many of which are described in Mahayana Buddhist literature.

55. This business about death refers both to physico-mental disintegration of one bonebag and also to so-called great death or esoteric death of conditioning in which one opens up and is helpless without ingrained strength in the awesome absence of customary defenses. Proper environment and companionship is thought to be helpful in transforming these experiences into truly liberating impacts.

56. Knot of substance, cluster of substance—'substance' here can mean element, inherent nature, thingness, body, essence. These refer to the substance of the universe, the essence of all things, thusness itself. This includes both the microcosmic aspect—the body—and the macrocosmic aspect—the world, universe, cosmos. Sengchao wrote, "Heaven, earth, and I have the same root; myriad things and I have one body." In itself it is beyond the grasp of human intellect, except indirectly; part can reflect the whole, but never exclusively contain it.

57.   This seems to refer to *parinirvana*, ultimate quiescence, at physical death.

58.   Prince of Dharma is the esoteric rank of the ninth stage of bodhisattvahood according to the teaching of the *Mahavastu;* the tenth is then consecration or anointment as king of Dharma. In the grand Avatamsaka description of fifty-two stages, these would be the nineteenth and twentieth, the highest of the so-called ten stations. As usual Pai-chang does not use the term strictly within any definition, but as the culmination of a personal search and effort, the blossoming of the awakened state of mind and merging with the world just as a sage king should identify with his people and land to share the benefits of kingship with them.

59.   In ancient Buddhism these were defined as the highest nonreturners (the third stage of sanctification), who progress through heavenly states engendered by their meditation, eliminating residual delusions. In Ch'an the term is used to suggest advanced students, progressive in the sense that they do not abandon themselves to complacency once they have realized inner peace, but continue to realize enlightenment everywhere.

60.   The *Heart Scripture* calls *prajnaparamita* ("transcendence of wisdom") the peerless spell.

61.   "Protect and remember." In the introduction to the *Lotus Scripture* it says, "The teaching of the great vehicle is expounded to those dedicated to enlightenment; it is called the scripture of infinite meaning, the principles of those dedicated to enlightenment, which the enlightened ones keep in meditation."

62.   This again pervades the microcosm and macrocosm, representing a human bodymind and its environment, all composed of impersonal elements, all ultimately equal and just as they are, thus. Subjectively, 'phenomena' means conceptions or the conceptual field, which coordinates data from the other senses into a sense of a unified

phenomenon or event. Buddhist psychology defines yet a seventh mind function beyond these which in its unregenerate state takes the data of the six senses through the sixth and assesses it based on an assumption of seer and seen or otherness and selfness, the selfness of others and otherness of self; transmuted, or "reborn", as it is called in Pure Land Buddhism, the so-called seventh consciousness becomes the awareness of equality.

63.   The ocean of worlds described in the *Avatamsaka* [Flower garland scripture], said to be lotus born and adorned by the deeds and practices vowed by Vairocana, the universal sun Buddha, the cosmic illuminator. Esoterically, Vairocana is the mind and his world is the field of mind.

64.   This has a different meaning in Mahayana Buddhism than in elementary Buddhism; here it means staying in personal nirvana, never coming out of absorption, forever detached and quiescent, without realization of emptiness and selflessness of things, forced to choose between stillness and confusion.

65.   Twenty-five states of existence refer to all realms from hells and animals to the highest heavens and formless absorptions. These are descriptions of psychological states insofar as they depend on the experiencer to exist. When Pai-chang speaks of things or realms which exist or do not or whatever, he is not only talking about realms of imagination or concrete reality as we conceive it, but is putting his point across in spite of what one may believe or think ontologically or epistemologically about whether anything exists objectively.

66.   Sovereignty in the world is said to be the destiny of a future Buddha if he doesn't renounce the attachments of home and social life.

67.   The ten virtues are not killing, no adultery, not lying, not reviling, not speaking with a forked tongue, not

speaking in a flattering or suggestive or otherwise improper manner, not greeding or lusting, not being angry, not entertaining false views. In the *Pao-en ching* [Scripture on requiting debt] II, a wheel-turning king says of himself, "Because I have no world-transcending law to benefit all living beings, although they ask and receive good things from me and hopefully gain security and happiness, yet in reality I cannot get them across the ocean of suffering" (*Taisho* 3, 132b). This is why the station of kingship or mundane power is inferior to Buddhahood. In Pai-chang's play on "wheel-turning," the wheel of dharma is equated with the wheel of karma; the mind becomes the wheel turner when it gets involved in routines, habitual attachments.

68.   "Four things"—food, clothing, shelter/bedding, medicaments.

69.   "Four kinds of birth in six dispositions"—beings born of womb, egg, moisture, or transformation, as hell beings, hungry spirits, animals, titans, humans, or gods. These are all said to exist in the realm of desire.

70.   In the third book of the *Lotus Scripture* it says, "If there is a hearer who rejoices in accord, know that this person will not regress." In the eighteenth book, entitled "The Merit of Rejoicing in Accord (with the teachings of the scripture)," it says that if someone hears the scripture, rejoices in accord, and preaches even one verse of it to others, and those others preach it to yet others, when it reaches the fiftieth person by this process, if that person rejoices, it is said that the merit of virtue of that person exceeds the virtue of a donor who nourishes all sentient beings and eventually brings them to liberation, exceeds the virtue of those who attain sainthood, the six powers, the three knowledges, and eight liberations upon hearing this teaching.

71.   Maya, whose name means "illusion," was the mother of Buddha (no enlightenment without illusion). According to *Pao-en Ching* III, her prayer was, "I made offerings to these five hundred self-enlightened sages, set

up monuments and made offerings to their relics—this merit I turn over to all beings, so that in future lives I will not have to give birth to so many children who are unable to conceive the spirit of enlightenment, leave society, and realize omniscience in the present lifetime." (*Taisho* 3, 140c) The personal extinction of suffering aimed at by the two vehicles does not compare to the bodhisattvas' acceptance of the nonproduction of all things.

72. In the *Lotus Scripture* the Buddha is likened to a king who gives away his crown jewel to his valiant sons who have successfully fought off the armies of demons. The jewel is the knowledge and perception of enlightenment. Pai-chang is saying one must see one's own empty nature; the profundity of inherent reality is its emptiness—only with this clear insight can one avoid attachment to virtue and knowledge.

73. The excrement is mental fabrication, meaningless conception. The metaphor comes from the *Lotus Scripture* IV, where a prodigal son is anonymously hired by his unrecognized rich father to clean out excrement. After a long time the son is taken more into his father's confidence and favor, but never presumes on this and remains humble; finally it is revealed that he is the true heir. This symbolizes those of the lesser vehicle, who after giving up wandering and spending years at purification are ready to be introduced to the way of complete enlightenment.

74. Another version reads, "If you seek Buddha (there) you're wrong," or "If you seek Buddha, that's not it." The ornaments are virtues and sciences; the thirty-two marks are signs of the ideal beatific Buddha body. Seeking with the sense of something to attain poses a barrier insurmountable on its own terms.

75. *Mahavaipulya;* the name of this branch of the canon is understood in Chinese to mean universal and equal, referring, for one thing, to the teaching of essential emptiness pervading all phenomena. According to the analysis of the T'ien-t'an school, this was the third period of Bud-

dha's teaching, in which he began to turn beings from the lesser vehicle towards the greater vehicle. Scriptures in this category include *Vimalakirtinirdesa* and *Lankavatara*.

76.   See footnote 27 for the four stages of meditation and eight absorptions. "Mental images" refers to *samjna*, perceptions or/and conceptions; these can be second or third generation reflexes of the immediate situation, or wholly constructed in meditation based on the energy and knowledge expressed in ancient tradition for communion with the source, or more creatively for a new generation. Focus without images produces the mirror-like effect which Ch'an masters used to eliminate discriminations based on mere habit; the mirror awareness metaphor may be carried further by referring to both the front and back of the mirror, the so-called great revival and great death. Pai-chang calls the mirrorlike consciousness the elixir of immortality, but it is not to be drunk all the time—the normal functions of human intelligence and feeling, freed from former bonds and compulsions, can resume in the wayfarer, but since he has access to the elixir he is no longer overwhelmed or totally compelled by mundane events. In the world of form, where meditation begins, there is no emotional involvement in discernment and reason.

77.   Meditational perceptions could be visualizations, ideas that come to one in meditation, or, perhaps more mundanely, ideas about the nature or process of meditation, or the conception that one is involved in such and such a meditation. Thusness meditation, called clear and pure, is sometimes considered the ultimate, being fundamental, behind and beyond any vision; but evolving succession, the so-called ancestral Ch'an, like the tantra of the diamond vehicle, being an active expression of enlightenment, was considered to that extent beyond the meditation in which one realizes thusness by oneself.

78.   Mahabhijnanabhibhu (whose name is invoked semantically in Chinese) was an ancient Buddha told of in

the *Lotus Scripture* in the chapter on the illusory citadel; when he had defeated the armies of demons (delusions) and was about to realize perfect enlightenment, still the attributes of all Buddhas (such as general and particular omniscience) did not become manifest in him—he sat with body and mind still for ten short aeons, yet the reality of enlightenment was not apparent to him. The gods of various heavens prepared a lion's throne for him under the tree of enlightenment; when he sat there, the kings of the pure (Brahma) heavens showered flowers for ten more short aeons; then the qualities of all the Buddhas became manifest in him, all their teachings were revealed to him, and he finally attained perfect enlightenment.

It is by not dwelling in the "illusory citadel" of nirvana that Buddhas and bodhisattvas serve as fields of blessings for sentient beings.

79. The lump of flesh on a Buddha's forehead, one of the thirty-two major marks of a great man, is said to be invisible to humans and gods, and is called the formless mark.

80. The six dispositions or states of being in the realm of desire: hell, hungry ghost, animal, titan, human, god.

81. The latest of the "seven Buddhas of antiquity" was Shakyamuni; Manjusri represents wisdom. The intent of this passage seems to be that Buddhahood is pictured as a remote development to avoid presumption, but true wisdom transcends all appearances and destroys the illusion of outward quest.

82. These figurative mountains enclose the eight hot hells; between them it is said there is no light. Representing the realm of ignorance, it is here that Manjusri's wisdom and guidance are really needed.

83. *Cintamani*, the magical, wish-fulfilling gem, is often used to symbolize free mind.

84. In the pure land Sukhavati of Amitabha Buddha,

it is said that one's feet are supported by precious lotus flowers or lotus leaves.

85. The ability to divide or reproduce the body is one of the powers attributed to a Buddha. Instances of people appearing in two places at one time are not particularly rare in mystic annals, but such powers are seldom given credence in ordinary society, certainly not to the extent that they are depicted in Buddhist scriptures. All beings and personalities can be seen as reflections of transhistorical Buddhas, bodhisattvas, and Buddha lands, but Paichang here describes the process of emanation or division of the body as merely the free ranging of the thoughts and acts of the liberated mind, indeed, as the particularization of the elemental cosmos itself.

86. In the eleventh book of the *Lotus Scripture,* a shrine appears, revealing an ancient Buddha who comes to life to expound the Dharma, sharing his seat with Shakyamuni. This scene is a popular theme in Buddhist art.

87. Fire and water represent hate and love or rage and lust.

88. This is from the third book of the *Scripture Spoken by Vimalakirti,* in the section on Subhuti; it refers to nonattachment to the sense of righteousness, impartiality in all things.

89. The term "jackal" is usually associated with having a sense of attainment; it is said that "the roar of a lion can burst the brain of a jackal," where the "lion's roar" is that of absolute emptiness, devoid even of emptiness, where there is no sense of attainment as acquisition.

90. Hui-neng, the sixth patriarch, said, "If you do not think at all and always keep thoughts cut off, this is bondage by Dharma; it is called a biased view."

91. There is a saying in a scripture, echoed by Lin-chi, that even if there were anything surpassing nirvana, it would just be a dream and an illusion.

92. The conclusion of the *Heart Scripture* says, "This is the great spiritual charm, this is the great enlightening charm, this is the unexcelled charm, this is the peerless charm." This refers to the transcendence of wisdom.

93. In the eleventh book of the *Lotus Scripture*, on the appearance of the monument, the Buddha changes the world into a pure land; this represents the attainment of discipleship, the culmination of which is sainthood. Next he changes an immense number of other worlds into pure lands; this represents the attainment of self-enlightenment or so-called solitary Buddhahood. Finally he changes another immense number of other worlds into pure lands; this represents the attainment of the unitary vehicle, the way of complete enlightenment and universal Buddhahood. Various explanations of these three transformed pure lands are made by different commentators on the *Lotus*. The Buddha purified the lands, removed hells, animals, hungry ghosts, titans and gods, because he wanted to reassemble all the reproduced or emanated Buddhas, to hear the Dharma expounded by the ancient Buddha Prabhutaratna. This represents a principle theme of the *Lotus*, awakening sentient beings to their common enlightened nature, to vision and knowledge of eternal reality. Titans, or anti-gods, are mainly concerned with personal power and whatever indulgences it can command; because of the waning of their own estate and the rise of others, they are usually characterized by anger. What is titanic about them is their egoism, their sense of self and other.

94. *Saindhava* can mean salt, water, a vessel, or a horse; the wise interpret the meaning according to the situation. See *Mahaparinirvana sutra* IX, *Blue Cliff Record* 92.

95. The six senses or the six superknowledges.

96. This is from a verse on "The Nonduality of Quietude and Disturbance," attributed to Pao-chih, "Master Chih" (418–514), a well-known living bodhisattva who lived in southeast China during the six dynasties era. As

recorded in the classic Ch'an history *Ching-te chuan-teng lu* 29, it reads, "Disciples dislike noise and seek quiet; that's like throwing away flour seeking cake. Cake is originally flour; there are a hundred variations in what is made, according to the person. Affliction is identical to enlightenment; without mind, there is no object. Birth and death does not differ from nirvana; greed and anger are like flames, like shadows. The wise have no mind to seek Buddha; fools cling to the false and the true. If you toil uselessly wasting your whole life, you don't see the wonderful crown of the realized one. If you realize that the nature of lust is empty, boiling water in the cauldron and embers in the stove are cool of themselves."

97. The four gross elements, representing the components of existence, are earth, water, fire, and air. Wind is air, and is associated with movement; fire and water represent rage and lust, earth is associated with gravity and depression. Zen Master Bunan (17th C.) said, "The deluded are used by their bodies; the enlightened use their bodies."

98. The three states or stages—detachment, nonabiding in detachment, nonintellectualization of nonabiding—have been more fully explained before; beyond this, according to Pai-chang, is Buddhahood, where everything one sees and experiences is like a reflection of the cosmic Buddha Vairocana, the primal illuminator, and everything one thinks, says, or does, is a reflection of the primordial Buddha or enlightened nature within oneself as within all beings. As Pai-chang points out, this is not acquired, so the notion of cause should not be absolutized; yet something is needed to make it manifest, to actually end the defiled, hypocritical mind, so the notion of naturalness should not be absolutized either.

99. According to the analysis of the Fa-hsiang ("characteristics of things") school of Buddhist philosophy, there are five natures of potentialities which sentient beings may have: those with the fixed nature of disciple,

self-enlightened one, or bodhisattva, who have the respective potentials for sainthood, solitary Buddhahood, or complete Buddhahood; then there are those of indefinite nature, who may become saints or Buddhas, and those of no nature, with no potential for enlightenment. In true Mahayana Buddhism the last category is not recognized as fixed; according to Ch'an teaching, the fixedness or fluidity of one's "nature" in this respect must be taken as one's own responsibility.

100.   "Unborn and imperishable" is an epithet of nirvana, also of the enlightened mind; it is called impermanent (or it is said that the Buddhas pass away) to avoid presumption on the everpresent enlightened nature once the teaching "mind is Buddha" is consciously known.

101.   The Evil One (Papiyan), king demon, personifies greedy mind; the six heavens of desire are the six senses.

102.   This alludes to a story in the *Lotus Scripture*, and means getting rid of mental fabrications about the nature of reality, a task of the first stage of Buddhist practice.

103.   The classic *Pao-ching san-mei-ke*, [Song of the jewel mirror concentration] by the famous ninth-century Ch'an master Tung-shan Liang-chieh says, "Turning away or touching are both wrong, for it is like a mass of fire."

104.   Once when Gautama Buddha's disciples were anguished over their past faults and unable to attain realization, Manjusri (embodiment of transcendent wisdom) drew a sword as if to kill the Buddha. The sense of righteousness and guilt alike are manifestations of self-importance. This story comes from the *Maharatnakuta Scripture*, in the chapter on the assembly of emperors suitably dwelling in their rank (*Taisho* 11, 590b). Pai-chang emphasized detachment from "impure things" first, then detachment from "pure things" afterwards.

        Angulimalya (or Angulimalika) became the object of love of his teacher's wife, incurring false accusation and the anger and hatred of his teacher. The teacher then gave Angulimalya a false teaching in revenge, claiming that killing people sends them right into nirvana, extinction of suffering and perfect peace. Angulimalya became a madman who murdered people and cut off their fingers to adorn his cap (his name represents this in Sanskrit). When at last he was about to kill his own mother, he was awakened by the Buddha. Finally the Buddha reveals that Angulimalya had already realized the Way in another world, that the teacher, his wife, and Angulimalya's parents were all just illusory players in a didactic performance. This Angulimalya appears in several texts, including minor scriptures bearing his name.

105. Five crimes against humanity which bring immediate and unrelieved retribution are parricide, matricide, shedding the blood of a perfectly enlightened one, breaking up the harmonious community, and destroying scriptures and images of enlightened ones and saints. Sometimes killing saints is specifically mentioned as well. The mystic interpretation alluded to by Pai-chang is described by his spiritual grandson Lin-chi as follows: "Ignorance is father—your momentary mental impulse. When you look for where it originates and ends, you cannot find it; it is like an echo answering the void. Having no concerns with anything wherever you may be is called killing your father." "Greed is your mother—your momentary impulse entering into the realm of desire. When you look for greed and lust, you only see the empty character of all things; having no attachment anywhere is called killing your mother." "What is shedding the blood of a Buddha?" "In the pure realm of reality, when you do not conceive a single thought of understanding, then everywhere is dark—this is shedding the blood of Buddha." "What is breaking up the harmonious community?" "In an instant of thought you realize that afflictions, compulsion and bondage are like space and have no basis; this is breaking up the harmonious community." "What is burning scriptures and images?" "Seeing the causal nexus is empty, mind is empty, space is empty, instantly transcending with

utter certainty, beyond all things—this is called burning scriptures and images" (*Lin-chi lu*, shih-chung 14). A similar motif is found in the *Scripture Spoken by Vimalakirti* and the sayings of the ninth-century Ch'an master Ts'ao-shan Pen-chi, a younger contemporary of Lin-chi, Yang-shan, Tung-shan, and other great teachers. The technique of taking ancient stories or themes and "picking them up sideways and using them upside down" is used in some Mahayana scriptures as well as in the works of the commentators and patriarchs of the so-called doctrinal schools, and is very common in Ch'an writings and sayings. Earlier Pai-chang referred to remaining in the highest absorptions in the immaterial realm as a grievous error, shedding the Buddha's blood, blocking the light of enlightenment.

106.   The six ways of transcendence are generosity, morality, tolerance, energy, meditation, and wisdom. Added to this are technical skills for liberation, power, knowledge, and will, to make ten transcendences.

107.   Being offered a canopy represents the highest stage of bodhisattvahood, according to the *Mahavastu*, called "consecration" as a king of Dharma.

108.   Vairocana, also known as the Great Sun, is the primordial illuminator, the source and basis of all according to esoteric Buddhism.

109.   This is the so-called repository or storehouse consciousness, which contains all the impressions from which the world as we know it comes to be. See the appendix on the analysis of consciousness.

110.   Locana is a name for the *sambhogakaya*, "body of reward," the state of enjoyment of the results of cultivation. The *dhyani* (meditation) Buddhas visualized by cultivators of esoteric Buddhism may be said to be reward-body Buddhas; the bliss of their pure lands is a "reward" of transcending mundane joys and sorrows, pleasures and pains.

111. In the fifty-two states of bodhisattvahood described by the Hua-yen scripture are included ten stages of faith, ten of abiding, ten of action, ten of dedication, ten of bodhisattvahood, plus universal and inconceivable enlightenment.

112. Tu-shun (558-640) was the first patriarch of Hua-yen studies in China. He is often quoted in Ch'an texts, and was popularly believed to have been a manifestation of Manjusri, the bodhisattva of pure wisdom.

113. The realm of form is the material realm, except that (outside of its definition as one of the five clusters of mortal being) it is extended to include so-called inner form or mental images. Below this is the realm of desire; so "giving up" images and desires is medicine. Above this is the immaterial or formless realm, where the highest meditational absorptions range—infinities of space, consciousness, nothingness, and neither perception nor nonperception. This passage refers to practice.

114. Some Ch'an masters did not travel much before or after meeting their real teacher; some traveled extensively, but it seems from the records and admonitions of some masters, some students left too soon to wander from one place to another without the capacity to benefit fully from meetings with adepts. Ananda is traditionally cited in Ch'an as one whose fondness for learning delayed his realization.

115. The three illuminations are knowledge of past lives, clairvoyance (divine eye), and knowledge of nonindulgence. The six superknowledges include these, and add clairaudience (divine ear), mental telepathy, and travel by will.

116. Unhindered understanding of things (or teachings), their principles, their expressions, and eloquence in explanation.

117. The vows to deliver all beings, cut off all afflic-

tions, study all approaches to the truth, and to fulfill the way of universal enlightenment.

118. The absolute and relative, or ultimate and conventional realities.

119. The image of the scent-bearing elephant comes from the *Mahaparinirvana sutra* [Scripture of the great decease]. "Scent-bearing" means "in the heat of passion," "in rut." This seems to say that intellectual passions can be as much a binding affliction as emotional passions can be, even more so because of their sometimes subtle nature.

120. In the sixth book of the *Scripture Spoken by Vimalakirti* (the section on wonders), it says a bodhisattva abiding in unconceivable liberation can pick up a world system as if it were a potter's wheel, put it in the palm of his hand and hurl it beyond myriad worlds, yet the beings therein would be unaware of going anywhere. Again he can return it to its original place, all without causing people to have any notion of going or coming, and the original features of the world would be the same as before.

121. The lion's roar is a conventional symbol for the real Buddhist teaching, the teaching of absolute emptiness, in which there is nothing gained as an object.

122. The eight winds ("influences") are profit, loss, vilification, praise, fame, censure, pain and pleasure. These winds stir the mind and cause the flame of wisdom to flicker unless it is protected by meditational stability.

123. The simile of yellow leaves presented as gold to a child to stop its crying appears in the *Mahaparinirvana Scripture* XX. Yang-shan said, "You people should each turn back your own light and reflect; do not memorize my words. Since beginningless aeons you have turned your backs on illumination and plunged into darkness; the roots of your false conceptions are deep and hard to pull out all at once. Therefore we temporarily set up expedient methods to take away your coarse consciousness; this is like using yellow leaves to put an end to crying" (*Transmission of the Lamp* II).

124.   Mahayana scriptures like the *Diamond Cutter* and the *Lotus of Reality* extol the virtue of accepting and upholding even a four-line stanza of the scripture; the scriptures glorify the widespread communication of the teachings, but also, as in the Ch'an school, take this to mean actual application of the teachings to oneself, not just recitation or explanation.

125.   The four attainments, as defined early on in Buddhism, are stream enterer, once returner, nonreturner, and saint. See note 30 on stream enterers. A once returner returns once to mundane life before final liberation, and a nonreturner remains in a so-called "heaven of pure abodes" until passing away utterly. Saints are *arhats*, "worthies," who realize nirvana in this very life. A Buddha is known as a great saint.

126.   Greed, lust, defilement, anger, clinging, dwelling, dependence, attachment, grasping, and affection.

127.   The three causal bases of enlightened nature are 1) the true basis, which is the enlightened (Buddha) nature inherent in everyone, 2) the basis of comprehension, which is the wisdom which intuitively realizes enlightened nature, and 3) the basis of conditions, or affinity, the practices designed to awaken wisdom. These three are compared to gold in the mind, knowledge of its existence there, and the processes of mining and smelting. Nanch'uan said, "The basis of comprehension does not exist by way of seeing, hearing, or conscious knowledge; perception and knowledge are in the realm of conditioning, and only exist when counterposed with things. This spiritual subtlety is inconceivable and has no object" (*Ku-tsun-su yu-lu* [Records of sayings of ancient adepts]).

128.   The eight aspects of attainment to the Way represent the career of Shakyamuni or any idealized *nirmanakaya* (manifestation-body) Buddha. There are slightly

differing versions, but they are generally the same: descent from the Tushita heaven, conception, birth, leaving society, conquering demons, attaining the Way, expounding the truth, and entering parinirvana.

129.   Chunda was a smith who gave Shakyamuni Buddha the food which poisoned him and occasioned his death. According to legend, the Buddha knew what would happen, and told his disciples not to eat the food, of which he alone partook. He also told them to allay Chunda's remorse on the grounds that the two most worthy offerings to a Buddha are that after eating which he becomes enlightened, and that after eating which he dies and enters parinirvana. A Buddha, or Realized One, is not a "body of mixed food" because he has transcended self and the individual body and realized thusness, merging with the body of reality.

130.   Shakyamuni is said to have sat for six years in the Himalayas before realizing enlightenment.

131.   This is taken from Seng-chao's *Pan-jo wu-chih lun* [Wisdom has no knowledge]. Here Seng-chao says that transcendental wisdom has no knowledge, properly speaking, because it has no object as such. These brief quotations by Pai-chang are all aimed at the basic practices for ending habitual illusion and awakening pure wisdom without object.

132.   "Sharing concerns" or "doing the same things" is one of the four unifying methods, or social practices, of bodhisattvas traditionally defined in Mahayana Buddhism. The others are giving, or generosity, loving speech, and beneficial action.

Thomas Cleary holds a doctorate in East Asian languages and civilizations from Harvard University, and has published several other translations of classical Zen teachings, including the *Blue Cliff Record*, *Timeless Spring: An Anthology of Soto Zen*, and Dogen's *Shobogenzo Zuimonki*.